What People Are Saying About:
The 10-Step Empowerment Series

"Through the use of introspective questions the book invites the reader to take a journey of self examination in order to accept the loss and to reengage in life."

—Ian Landry, MA, MSW, Case Manager

"Bevan has real-life experience in the area of loss and 'rebuilding' her life and self-esteem in the face of traumatic experiences such as being abandoned by a partner."

—Margaret M. Mustelier, Psy.D.

"Nowadays there are too many books about adult loving relationships, but they usually are generic and abstract descriptions. This book is different because it moves to specificity and provides concrete steps to overcome a disrupting episode in our lives."

—Carlos J. Sanchez, MA, Family Therapist

"Lynda Bevan delivers what she promises in the title of the book: it is a practical guide and a no-nonsense approach. Her descriptions of the experiences are palpable."

—Chin Tao, LMFT

"This is a well thought out, useful little book that is an excellent guide for those recovering from a broken long-term relationship."

—Robert Rich, MSc, PhD, M.A.P.S.,

"The book is studded with illuminating case studies and provides an excellent exposition of issues such as post-traumatic emotional responses, pre-trauma expectations, setting boundaries, forgiveness and acceptance, and the do's and don'ts of moving forward. A gem."

—Sam Vaknin, PhD
author *Malignant Self Love: Narcissism Revisited*

"Bevan provides practical steps to help a person begin the process of change, and during that process, to decide how the relationship will be affected, and whether to stay in the relationship, based on how your partner reacts to your new behaviors."

—Tyler R. Tichelaar, PhD
Author of *The Marquette Trilogy*

"This easy to relate to, solution-focused guide does not attempt to push an agenda; it simply provides a foundation of understanding along with the tools necessary to begin trusting one's own feelings again.. Bevan dedicates great thought towards realistic problem solving approaches while maintaining a focus on safety, health, and growth."

—Erin M. Hudges, LCSW
Rebecca's Reads

"I truly feel that every individual who is dealing with issues of some form of jealousy will greatly benefit from reading *Life Without Jealousy* by Lynda Bevan. This includes people who are not jealous themselves but are being affected by others who are. Learning to understand it, overcome it, and gain effective new ways to communicate will greatly improve the quality of our lives."

Paige Lovitt
—*Reader Views*

LIFE
Without
BULLYING

A
PRACTICAL
GUIDE

Lynda
Bevan

THE 10-STEP EMPOWERMENT SERIES

Life Without Bullying: A Practical Guide

Book #3 in the 10-Step Empowerment Series

Copyright © 2012 by Lynda Bevan. All Rights Reserved.

First Edition: January 2012

Originally published under the title *Stop Being Pushed Around: A Practical Guide*

Library of Congress Cataloging-in-Publication Data

Bevan, Lynda.
  Life without bullying : a practical guide / Lynda Bevan. -- 1st ed.
    p. cm. -- (10-step empowerment series)
  Includes bibliographical references and index.
  ISBN-13: 978-1-61599-150-1 (trade paper : alk. paper)
  ISBN-13: 978-1-61599-151-8 (ebook)
  1. Bullying Prevention Program. 2. Bullying--Prevention. 3. Man-woman relationships. I. Title.
  BF637.B85B48 2008
  158.2--dc22
                          2007046330

Published by:
Loving Healing Press
5145 Pontiac Trail
Ann Arbor, MI 48105
USA

Distributed by Ingram (USA/CAN), Betram's Books (UK)

http://www.LovingHealing.com or
info@LovingHealing.com
Fax +1 734 663 6861

Loving Healing Press

Table of Contents

THE 10-STEP EMPOWERMENT SERIES

- Life After Your Lover Walks Out
- Life After Betrayal
- Life Without Bullying
- Life Without Jealousy
- Overcoming Guilt

About our Series Editor, Robert Rich, Ph.D.

Loving Healing Press is pleased to announce Robert Rich, Ph.D. as Series Editor for the *10-Step Empowerment Series*. This exciting new series conveys practical guides written by seasoned therapists for solving real-life problems.

Robert Rich, M.Sc., Ph.D., M.A.P.S., A.A.S.H. is a highly experienced counseling psychologist. His web site www.anxietyanddepression-help.com is a storehouse of helpful information for people suffering from anxiety and depression.

Bob is also a multiple award-winning writer of both fiction and non-fiction, and a professional editor. His writing is displayed at www.bobswriting.com. You are advised not to visit him there unless you have the time to get lost for a while.

Three of his books are tools for psychological self-help: *Anger and Anxiety: Be in charge of your emotions and control phobias, Personally Speaking: Single session email therapy,* and *Cancer: A personal challenge.* However, his philosophy and psychological knowledge come through in all his writing, which is perhaps why three of his books have won international awards, and he has won many minor prizes. Dr. Rich currently resides at Wombat Hollow in Australia.

Introduction

Are you a victim? Are you living with a victim? This book is for you if you can answer yes to one of these questions.

Reading on will help you to understand the thinking process of a victim and will assist you in transferring from the role of victim to the role of survivor. Following this plan will enable you to do this by clearly identifying how you became a victim and how you can change your thinking and behavior patterns in order to embrace the role of survivor.

If you are a victim or living with one, you will know that to have a relationship with a victim is hard work and an uphill struggle in that it drains you of energy and places responsibility and accountability on to one person in the partnership, the survivor. The relationship that exists for you at the present time is difficult because one of you is negative. This person refuses to take responsibility for all input—whether it is emotional or physical.

By reading this book, and adopting the strategy of changing your role, you will experience the highs and lows of changing yourself. It is necessary but difficult to relive the past in order to find out how and why you became a victim in the first instance, but the eventual reward is worth your effort as you relinquish the victim role and adopt the role of survivor.

1 | Are You a Victim?

Definitions of Victim

- An unfortunate person who suffers from some adverse circumstance
- A person who is tricked or swindled
- Someone who has suffered from an unlawful act, whether it is a personal or a property crime
- A person harmed by another's action
- A person on whom sexual violence is inflicted
- Someone who suffers some loss as a result of another's action
- An individual who suffers direct or threatened physical, emotional, financial, or spiritual harm as a result of a crime/domestic abuse.

We shall examine the role of] will look at the role of "victim" in adult marriage/partnership relationships and will explain how to change the role from "victim" to "survivor". In Appendix A, we expand this model to include workplace bullying.

You are a victim if...

- you believe that you have no control over your life
- you believe that you can do nothing right
- you believe that no-one really cares for you
- you are often negative
- you waiting for someone to rescue you

- you put pressure on you partner to make everything alright for you
- you opt out of life
- you are fearful
- your are insecure
- you are usually depressed or anxious
- you feel under constant threat of something bad happening
- you sabotage positive thinking and behavior
- you are distrustful
- you wait for disasters to occur
- you have emotional problems
- you may turn to drugs or alcohol as a means of escape
- you are isolated from friends and family
- you withdraw from real life

A 'victim' in a marriage/partnership relationship sucks and drinks the energy of the other member. A 'victim' is a 'bloodsucker' draining the partner of energy, enthusiasm and drive. 'Victims' are negative and/or can't be bothered to do anything constructive for themselves so they rely on a partner or anyone else to give them what they want at any cost. They will surrender control of their lives over to their partner in the hope that their partner will make everything alright.

A 'victim' needs to work hard to stay the same in order to prevent life changes. Victimhood is enabled by the partner doing things to help the victim. A 'victim' has taken a long time to become this way and will be extremely reluctant to surrender the role. If you are living with a 'victim' or are a 'victim' yourself, you will know that by opting out of responsibility and accountability you are, in effect, the controller of the relationship, albeit a negative controller.

To victimize someone is to persecute them. To victimize someone is also to 'pester' them. Slow and deliberate pestering can wear an individual down into an anxious/depressive state of mind. Pestering (nagging) is to persistently annoy someone into surrender.

> "When persecuting/victimizing someone, you are subjecting them to harassment designed to injure, grieve and afflict."(Merriam-Webster)

Example of Becoming a Victim

A lady I have counseled told me that she had tried, very hard, to mend her broken marriage with her husband. When they separated, she had moved out of the family home with her children and moved back to her mother's home nearby. The couple remained in touch daily. He visited her mother's home every weekend to spend quality time with his children. Eventually, both parties accepted the break-up but were eager that the children would not suffer unduly.

During this phase, they continued sleeping together on the weekend visits and generally behaved as if they were still in a marriage. My patient was happy with this situation because she wanted to reconcile and give the marriage a second chance. Her husband seemed happy with this arrangement and gave her all the signs that this is what he wanted also. This situation continued for some 18 months. As time moved on, however, this lady began to realize that she had become a victim of her husband's controlling behavior yet again.

The weekend typically began with her welcoming him into her mum's home on a Friday evening with a hearty meal, wine and the warmth of a loving family atmosphere. The following day he took the children on a daytrip and she never knew whether she would be invited to 'tag' along. She always was invited eventually, but the question always hung in the air until the last possible moment when he grudgingly agreed to her coming along, usually after a request from one of the children.

It dawned on her that even when they had lived together permanently, her views had still never been taken into consideration. Indeed, she told me that when the family embarked on a daytrip she was never allowed to suggest a place to visit. If she volunteered an opinion, he would say quite curtly, "No-one is interested in where you want to go, your opinion in unimportant."

She also recalled being told to keep her head down as she walked along the road while taking their newly born baby for a walk in the pram, as she was offending passers-by because she was so ugly. During the years she was married to him, he had brainwashed her into believing that she was not up to much and "lucky to have met and married him." Slow and persistent brainwashing had reduced her to believing she could make nothing of herself and her life and was, therefore, privileged and grateful to have him. She became a 'victim' because she did not have the confidence to stand up to her controlling husband.

This is an all too familiar story of how to become a victim.

If You Are A Victim...

- You believe you're at your partner's mercy
- You smile when you want to cry
- You pretend that everything is alright
- You tip-toe around your partner all the time (treading on egg shells)
- You will do your partner's bidding—no matter the consequence to yourself
- You give-up on yourself
- You experience suppressed anger and frustration
- You become nondescript
- You have a low self-esteem
- You block out emotions

- You believe you are unloved

- Your life is flat-lining

- You are depressed and/or anxious

- You opt out of all responsibility and accountability, preferring their partner to make decisions

> "If you had a friend who talked to you like you sometimes talk to yourself, would you continue to hang around with that person?"
>
> —Rob Bremer

Here are some examples of positive responses a victim can choose on how to deal with a controller:

- Take control of yourself and your life

- Don't be afraid to show your feelings: learn when it is appropriate to do this.

- Encourage open discussions, to enable you both to have a better understanding of each other's point of view.

- Realize you are never going to get it right, so stop trying to be perfect.

- Be reasonable, flexible and fair in your responses, but know when enough is enough: you will know when this happens by the feeling in your gut that screams—*stop.*

- Treat yourself kindly.

- Acknowledge how much you have achieved.

- Don't be afraid to recognize your needs, wants and desires—you have a right to them.

- Accept that you "can't have it all," but make sure you "get some."

- Take charge of yourself and know that any change you want to achieve in your life is up to you.

A negative controller is someone who...

- has usually been abused (emotionally/ physically) as a child
- has frustrations that turn into anger
- is jealous and possessive in relationships and lacks trust in people generally
- has deep-seated insecurity issues
- focuses on the relationship to the exclusion of family and friends
- views compromise as a weakness
- has an unacknowledged low self-esteem
- shifts blame on to other people
- places high demands on the partner in the relationship, mainly because they he/she had little or no control in their own life
- is moody and subject the victim to either being charming or cruel
- has learned to be this way in order to deceive others
- vents frustrations on the partner through a false identification of the partner with one of the controller's parents (usually the mother)

If you are a controller, here are ways that you get the upper hand and create a 'victim'

- By bullying your partner
- By manipulating your partner to get your own way
- By frightening you partner into submission

- By having a need to control your partner, situations and outcomes
- By shifting blame from yourself on to your partner
- By showing disrespect to your partner
- By criticizing your partner
- By sabotaging yourself or your partner

> "We almost always have choices, and the better the choice, the more we will be in control of our lives."
> —William Glasser

I will take each of these styles and explain them. As I have already explained "victim", I will proceed with "bullying". Another way to gain control in a relationship is to bully your partner into submission until they surrender all control of their life to you (they become a victim). Bullies are inferior, inadequate people. They pick on sensitive, vulnerable people in order to feel superior.

To bully someone is to abuse your power in the worst way possible. Slow, cunning and persistent bullying can make the most confident individual a "gibbering wreck". Bullies are predators, hunting to find their victims. Bullies never give up—hounding their victims until they completely surrender and have no self-worth or identity.

Example of Bullying

I once counseled a confident, articulate lady who was the victim of bullying. She told me that her friends were all surprised that she had become a victim to bullying from her husband. She was competent and able and holding down a responsible job. Despite these circumstances, she succumbed to bullying. At first, of course, she didn't recognize that she was being bullied. She believed that all suggestions and advice were well meant and she listened intently when given any guidance and direction by her husband. She realized she was being bullied when she saw the reaction from her husband when she didn't take the advice/suggestions offered.

She felt whittled down into carrying out his every demand by the fear that he would leave her. She loved her husband and wanted to be with him forever at whatever cost. This cost was high and she paid it: he ruled the roost. He called the tune and she danced to it. The constant fear hanging over her head was that if she didn't do as he said he was going to walk out of her life forever. She couldn't cope with the possibility of living her life without the man she loved and be alone forever. This lady lived a double life. In the work arena she was a confident, able person who people turned to for help and advice. At home, she was a servile 'yes' woman who did as she was told.

She did stand up for herself, on some occasions, but these were short-lived because the threatening reaction and outbursts of anger she experienced from her husband frightened her and quickly put her back into her 'rightful' place beneath him. This lady tried all options available to her to change her husband. It took years for her to realize and accept that with all the best will in the world, the only person you can change is yourself. She was scared to change herself for fear of finding out that he wouldn't love her if her behavior changed and she became her own person. All she wanted was an equal relationship with him. Eventually she had no option but to change some aspects of herself. She was becoming frustrated and grossly unhappy in the relationship and the choice became apparent that either she began the process of changing herself or ending the relationship she had fought so hard to keep. The process began and, thankfully, in the most part has proved successful.

Some negative reactions to being bullied are:

- To experience being demoralized
- To be intimidated
- To be embarrassed

- To feel humiliated
- To be ridiculed
- To be patronized
- To be criticized
- To be ignored or dismissed
- To be overruled

Some positive ways to respond to bullying are:

- Avoid or delay responding
- Refuse to give up and give in
- Respond with courage
- Stand up and be counted—a bully is a coward
- Realize the bully is a frightened, inadequate individual—not the threatening monster he/she appears to be
- Be responsible for who you are and what you say
- Ignore pubic humiliation attempts, other people recognize what's happening and the person is quickly identified as a 'bully' and disrespected and disliked
- Be strong and proud of who you are and what you have achieved
- Realize that you will be better off if the bully does leave you, because the bullying will stop
- **If you feel that the bullying is going to turn into violence—contact a responsible agency in Appendix B.**

> "Never be bullied into silence. Never allow yourself to be made a victim. Accept no one's definition of your life; define yourself."
> —Harvey Fierstein (1952 -)

Always Getting Your Own Way

This is the desire to have total control in the relationship and putting you first at any price: being totally selfish. This individual is frightened of losing total control. Such a person is scared that, if they are not in control of all situations and people nearest to them, their circumstances/life could change dramatically and they would be left 'high and dry'.

They have no basic self-respect or do not like themselves and believe they are not liked or respected by others and, therefore, they have a desperate need to stay in control in order to keep and preserve what they have. They feel that they are failures.

They manipulate those people closest to them by any method that works for them.

Here are some examples:
- Menacing behavior
- Coaxing and cajoling
- Luring you into a false sense of security
- Sulking
- Aggression
- Attacking
- Bribery
- Threatening
- Pretending to walk out, as if never to return to trigger a fear of abandonment in you
- Violent behavior (as in slamming doors, stamping around the house)
- Body language (large and looming over you)
- Accusing

- Blaming

- **Physical Violence (when this occurs, or if there is a strong probability of this happening in your relationship—contact a responsible agency in Appendix B)**

In my opinion, this type of person is only respected superficial acquaintances. This controlling type can be friendly, talkative and interesting in professional and social situations. It is only when someone oversteps the self-imposed boundaries of the controller that outsiders will spot that the person is intolerant, aggressive, rude and threatening.

Example: Some years ago I saw a patient who told me that his wife had forbidden him to visit his longstanding friend (he had been friends with this person for twenty years). The reason his wife had initially given was that she did not personally know his friend and had never been invited to visit him. She was angry and felt excluded from the relationship and, worse, accused him of having a homosexual relationship with his friend. She was very angry and aggressive while discussing this issue, which caused a major disruption in the household. While my patient could accept the point his wife made regarding feeling excluded from the long-standing friendship, he could not, and would not, accept the accusation that he was conducting a homosexual affair with his friend.

However, he discussed this issue with his friend and, despite the inexcusable remarks, an invitation was extended to her to "call in any time" for a chat. The woman refused the invitation because she felt that she was being fobbed off as no *definite* invitation date had been extended. My patient continued to see his friend (once/twice a week) popping in for a coffee and a chat. It was a ridiculous situation and he felt guilty doing something without his wife's knowledge. However, he felt he needed to make a stand on this issue.

On one occasion when he was visiting his friend, there was a knock at the door and his wife appeared on the doorstep. My patient's friend invited her in to his home for a coffee but she refused and was very hostile, angry and rude. She had called in to the friend's house on the pretence to tell her partner that she was going somewhere and would not return for a couple of hours. What she was actually doing was making her presence felt in the most threatening and intimidating manner. She left her husband in no doubt of the confrontation that was to follow later. She was, in other words, menacing him. My patient was totally embarrassed and fearful of the outcome. He had experienced this behavior many times from his wife, and had always made excuses for her and accommodated her outbursts. He loved his wife and wanted a successful marriage but he also wanted to "hang out" with his friend and be able to "shoot the breeze," occasionally, as they had done prior to his marriage.

It wasn't as if he went out for a drink with his friend and was meeting other people he had previously known. This situation totally disabled him, describing his reaction to the event as feeling "weak in the knees," having a dry mouth and unable to have a clear, logical thought in his head. He couldn't stay at the friend's house after this incident had occurred and left immediately following his wife in an attempt to offset the inevitable major argument that was to follow. This act of scurrying after his partner only added fuel to her fire as the wife then knew that her behavior had achieved its required result: to get her own way.

Negative Options In Dealing With Someone Who Always Wants To "Get Their Own Way."

- Do anything you want behind your partner's back
- Try and coax, cajole and beg your partner to agreeing with you
- Tell the truth at all times (in the full knowledge that the outcome will be anger), and put up with the consequences

- Enter into lengthy discussions about the innocence of your intentions (usually to no avail)

- Support your partner at any price

- Love the bully more, and dance to their tune, to show and prove you could never, or would not want to be, without them

- Give in and submit all the time

- Give up on having a life of your own

- Fight 'fire with fire' and retaliate with anger

Positive Options in Dealing with Someone Always "Getting Their Own Way."

- Be still—do not react—let them "run out of steam"

- Do not be provoked, whatever they say

- Stay in control of *yourself*

- Devise a plan of action (the outcome you want to achieve)

- Stay focused on what you want

- Say nothing, other than giving answers such as, "I am not responding to you because I don't know the answer yet, and can't give you the answer you want at this time."

- Continue, quietly and unobtrusively, to follow your own plan and do your own thing (this will give you confidence and raise your self-esteem)

- Encourage open and honest discussions during quiet, peaceful, relaxing times

- When there is an easy flow of conversation taking place between you, assess whether it might be an appropriate time to air an issue causing you concern, i.e. "when we argue I feel unable to respond to you be-

cause you shout and frighten me with your presence."
This admission, gently said and repeated over many
months, might eventually sink in and the other person
might decide to start listening and stop shouting.

- Decide to change yourself by taking small steps and
making small changes at first. This will provoke your
partner to responding to you in a different way. If this
is done slowly there will be a positive result as shown
in *My Way: How to Live in a Difficult Relationship*.
This guide is an empowering strategy for changes in
relationships.

- Decide to leave the relationship

2 Does Fear Control You?

Frightening Someone into Submission

When disagreements occur, the bully will use anger to get control and force someone into submission. The argument/discussion usually starts in a reasonable way, but very quickly spirals out of control. This happens when the controller sees a risk of losing the argument. Their voice becomes raised, their eyes bulge in their head, their face may flush red or become as white as a corpse. This person will loom over you and shout in your face. The bully resorts to disgusting behavior and language, spitting obscenities your way. These outbursts, over a period of time, brainwash the victim into believing they are worthless. The victim in this scenario is left baffled, lost for words, disabled and unable to respond. The victim is temporarily tongue-tied as the fear of the moment takes over and paralyzes them. The victim's only thought is to calm the person down and get out of the situation as soon as possible. It is a dreadful feeling that you desperately hope never happens again. Unfortunately, it always does.

The controller has deliberately resorted to anger to get their own way and to ensure that they won't be challenged about any issues in the future. They refuse to be challenged. If you challenge this type of individual—do it at your peril! This is the lowest form of interaction between people. It is bullying and it subjects another person to threats and possible violence unless they do what they are told. It is cowardly. It stems from an inability to discuss calmly, fairly and frankly the issue in hand for fear of losing the argument or discussion and also losing control of another person or set of circumstances. The type of person that behaves in this way really only cares about themselves.

They say they love you, of course they would say that, but do you really believe that someone who loves you would treat you in that way?

On the other hand, a controller who is in love is so afraid of losing that special person that they resort to unacceptable behavior in order to frighten them into staying with them. The home becomes a household ruled by threats and fears. A household should be ruled by love and compassion. Being on the receiving end of threatening behavior is fearsome. Being confronted with bulging eyes and a tight-lipped snarl is scary and would make most people submit. In my opinion, "A threat is a projected fear on the part of the person with the threatening behavior." If the person exposed to the threatening behavior can remember this during the time the anger explodes, then they might feel more able to deal with the outburst and react in a different way. The person threatening is the person who is scared and frightened and is projecting this fear on to their partner in the hope that the issue will go away. They make themselves angry, safe in the knowledge that their demonic persona will frighten the other person into total submission.

Here are some examples:

- When someone threatens to leave you if you do not comply with their demands

- When you feel forced to do something against your will

- When you are the subject of menacing behavior

- When your every move is criticized

- When you are constantly watched

- When you are constantly ridiculed

Examples of frightening someone into submission:

In my opinion, women are the most likely candidates for being victims of this type of control. Women are easier to frighten into submission than men, I believe (there are exceptions, of course).

One woman I saw, on a fairly regular basis, could recount story after story of, in her words, "having to submit to my husband's unreasonable behavior and demands." She didn't have to submit or respond to him—she knew that—she also knew the reason why she was giving in to him. She could not, and did not want to survive without him in her life. She believed that "life would be unbearable without him." She sabotaged herself. Her personality changed, her outlook on life changed, she put on weight, became unkempt in her appearance. She became anxious, depressed, and without hope for the future.

She totally accepted life on his terms. She was afraid to make a decision on her own. He even tried to interfere with, and tell her how to manage a very successful business she had built up on her own, before she had even met him. Such was his need to control his wife. It was sad to watch this lady in her unhappy state. She knew that in order to be free again and live a carefree life she had to let him go, but she couldn't do it. Her doctor prescribed antidepressants and, reluctantly, she accepted this in order to help her cope with living her chosen path. Her visits to me gave her the opportunity to unburden herself and tell an outsider of the quarrels and the situations that she was experiencing.

Her husband gave her no emotional or physical support at home. She did everything to keep the house going, i.e., cooked for the family, cleaned the house, did the laundry for the family (always ensuring that he had a clean shirt and socks or "war would be declared.") He, on the other hand, would come home from work, 'slob out' in front of the television, and that's where he would stay all evening. He would not budge an inch to get himself anything he might want, e.g. a drink, etc. The remote control would be at his side (or firmly gripped in his hand) and there he would be, in all his glory, controlling the entire household from his armchair.

She felt foolish telling me of these scenarios and kept repeating, "I know I should leave him, you must think I am stupid and deserve what I am getting." She would also say, and believe, "Perhaps I've done something in my past and I deserve the treatment I am getting." Despite firm reassurances from me that I did not believe that this was the case, she could not get these thoughts out of her mind. I urged her to continue coming to see me and, over a period of time, gently encouraged her to take back some control of her life by taking small steps to re-establish her self-respect.

By this time, her self-esteem had spiraled down so low that no amount of the 'talking therapies' would have worked alone. Shortly after being prescribed anti-depressants her energy levels began to rise and she was able to begin the journey of taking back some control of her life with regular counseling sessions.

Another story unfolded in a counseling session: A lady, who had been married for some 12 years, confided that there was a list of things that she could not do, at home, for fear of disapproval from her husband. These were:

- She cannot put nail polish on her nails as he does not like the smell; it gives him a headache, and he becomes angry if she does this

- She must not chew gum—he cannot stand the noise

- She must not make conversation, while out socializing, unless he likes the person she is speaking to

- He says she snores, or breathes too loudly, so he opts to sleep in the spare bedroom most nights

- She must not fall asleep in the chair in the living room in the evening. If she does this, he slams his hand down on the arm of the chair, or stamps his foot on the floor to awaken her (with a start)

- When they both go out for a meal and she chooses the table they sit at—he will always decide to sit somewhere elsewhere as her choice is unacceptable

Negative responses to being frightened into submission:

- Do as you are told at all times
- Never challenge your persecutor
- Jump when asked to do something
- Never share an idea or a thought
- Never voice your own opinion
- Accept that you are being totally controlled
- Accept your incapacity to change yourself and your situation
- Become anxious
- Become depressed
- Lead a stressful life

Positive responses to resist submitting to someone:

- Avoid responding and reacting
- Divert the conversation
- Challenge the controller
- Offer different options
- Realize they are cowards (knowing this, helps to take some fear away)
- Stop being afraid of them and know they are afraid of reaching an outcome they can't deal with
- Stay in reality and in the moment—don't be tempted to imagine an outcome that affects your future with this person
- If the other person threatens to leave you—don't be gullible and believe this—ask yourself has he/she ever left you before?

- Stay focused on your inner state of mind and body
- Hold yourself still inside
- **If you think the situation is going to spiral out of control and become violent—contact a responsible agency in Appendix B.**
- Smile, nod, agree and then do what you want to do
- Decide to change yourself
- Decide to change your responses
- Imagine you are someone else—how would they respond? If you discover appropriate reactions, try them
- Disengage emotionally (this can be achieved with practice, as below)
- Imagine you are the third person in the room—stay with that person (in your mind) and observe both yourself and your partner. This exercise will help you disengage from the emotional entanglement you have become involved in.
- See you partner for who he/she really is—"knowledge is power."

Controlling People, Situations and Outcomes

A controller always has to be the boss. They have to be admired and respected, and held in high esteem. They get this position by bullying and, usually, by holding the financial purse strings within a household. This person is obsessed with having their own way at all times. They believe that their thoughts, beliefs and actions are always right and should be adhered to by all the people within their rule. They are threatened by innovation, creativity and by someone who can 'hold their own' in social and professional situations. It is in the controller's interest to deliberately undermine any individual in their intimate circle who displays signs of being liked by others, getting ahead and becoming more successful than they are themselves. Controllers see themselves as supremely successful and liked by one and all. Really they are insecure, sad, failed individuals without any positive identity.

Here are some examples of control:

A patient visited me because she was experiencing severe control issues with her husband. One example of a controlling feature happened as they were both going out to the pub one evening. Prior to leaving the house my patient had made some sandwiches and placed them in the fridge in the full knowledge that her husband would be hungry upon returning home from the pub. During the drive to the pub, my patient realized that her husband was angry but could not understand why. Of course, she asked him and he replied, "You should know why." She racked her brain and could only come think of small, inconsequential reasons for his behavior. Nothing significant had happened to provoke him to behave in a disgruntled, rude, obnoxious manner.

When they arrived at the pub, they sat at the bar as they usually did. He ordered his drink but ordered nothing for her. The owner/bar-man (who knew them both as regular customers) guessed that there had been a disagreement and gave my patient her usual gin-and-tonic. Her husband then turned his back on her and totally ignored her for the entire evening. The owner of the pub was especially kind and understanding (incidentally, he was gay and emotionally sensitive and aware), and fed her drinks throughout the evening. Behind her husband's back, he quietly resorted to calling him rotten for treating her in that fashion.

When they returned home (the silence in the car was voluminous), she went to the fridge to give him the sandwiches she had prepared earlier. At this point she just wanted the evening to end. The children were in bed and she did not want to have a row that would wake and upset them. He didn't want the sandwiches and told her in a cold, threatening manner that he wanted scrambled eggs on toast. His words were, "go to the kitchen and make me scrambled eggs on toast." So, the servile being that she had become, she went out to the kitchen and made the scrambled eggs on toast.

When she returned to the living room with them on a tray, he looked at her in the most sinister way and told her he hadn't asked for scrambled eggs on toast, but that he'd asked for poached eggs on toast. He said, "Go back to the kitchen and make me poached eggs on toast." She went back to the kitchen and made poached eggs on toast and brought them back into the living room on a tray only to be told in a frighteningly dark, demonic way that he hadn't asked for poached eggs on toast he asked for fried eggs on toast. Again he said, "Go to the kitchen and make me fried eggs on toast."

So, she went back to the kitchen and was, by now, shaking in her shoes and scared stiff. She prayed that there were eggs left in the fridge. She wanted to grab the keys of the car and flee but couldn't because the children were upstairs in bed and she didn't want to leave them open to the possibility of being woken by her husband's ravings. There were eggs left in the fridge (thank God) and she made fried eggs on toast, and took them to the living room on a tray. When she presented this to him he said he had never asked for eggs in the first place—looked at her with complete disgust and contempt and went to bed.

She stayed downstairs for a long time and waited for him to drop off to sleep before venturing upstairs to the bedroom. In the morning, he behaved as if nothing had happened. He had exercised his masterful control, abused and bullied her to submission and was duly satisfied with the outcome. Of course he said he loved her.

Another example: Jill's father died from cancer several years ago, but still the ending had come suddenly and unexpectedly. At the time, Jill was married and had three small children. When the death occurred, and after discussion with her husband John, she stayed at her Mum's home a few miles away.

This allowed her to be with her Mum, accept visitors and to organize the funeral arrangements. Jill was away from her husband and children for four days. Finally, after the funeral Jill returned to her small family and began to relax for the first time since her Dad had passed away.

There had been no time for her to react to her Dad's passing as she had been busy making arrangements and comforting her Mum. When Jill and John went to bed that night, John wanted to make love to his wife. However, Jill felt unable to comply and confided in her husband that she had not had the time to come to terms with the death of her father and, having a vivid imagination, was worried that he might be standing at the bottom of the bed watching them having sex. John replied that it was OK, because he had been meaning to tell Jill that he had been having an affair for the past couple of years and didn't need her for sex anyway.

Negative responses to being controlled

- Do as you're told
- Never object to anything asked of you
- Be attentive at all times
- Put your needs at the bottom of the list
- Never expect anything
- Know your place
- Accept you are neither good enough or worthy to have an opinion or be listened to
- Be totally accountable to someone else
- Give in and give up on your wants, needs, desires

How to overcome being controlled in a relationship:

In my opinion, this will take a long time to overcome. In my book *My Way To Help You Live In A Difficult Relationship*, I have devised a 10 step guide to enable people to address this issue. I developed this strategy during the time that I was having problems within my relationship and have used this method with patients, during my career as a Counselor, with much success.

> "Do not let circumstances control you; you change your circumstances."
>
> —Jackie Chan

Shifting Blame from Yourself

The angry person is rarely wrong. You dare not disagree. Any of your suggestions are usually rejected by them. They are cunning and manipulative and get their own way by browbeating their nearest and dearest. When suggestions are repeated to someone regularly, however bizarre the suggestions are on a logical level, eventually you will begin to believe them. So, if you are told often enough that you are wrong and stupid, you will start to believe it and will stop making suggestions in the future for fear of looking stupid.

An angry person will always blame the other for pushing them into becoming angry. How many times have I heard patients tell me that their partner says, "It's your fault I am like this, you push me to the extreme and ask for all you get." Another repeating pattern of an angry person is to deny that they have said something that clearly they did. Have you witnessed this conversation? "I didn't say that," You reply, "You did," and repeat in detail not only the conversation that had taken place, but where you both were the time and date and what you were wearing at the time. Hot denial follows hot denial, eventually culminating in another outburst of anger. It is the angry person's way of stopping you in your tracks. They will not accept responsibility or accountability for their statements, actions or reactions, unless, of course, it suits them to do so.

Examples:

1. Nora confided that she was even afraid to suggest a place to visit for a holiday, in the full knowledge that if the holiday destination was disappointing, she would be blamed and punished for the duration of their stay. Nora wouldn't give an opinion on what or where they would like to go on an evening out because they knew that if the evening turned out to be bad in any way, she would be blamed. The same pattern occurred if they wanted to watch a television program that turned out to be uninteresting to her partner. She would be blamed for making the wrong selection. Nora succumbed to agreeing with the partner's plans regarding any socializing, television programs and future holidays—in order for peace to reign in the partnership.

2. Nora also told me that during an argument, her partner Mark would voice his opinions vociferously on a particular point and hammer it home. Nora dared not argue with Mark at that time, so she would just agree for "peace at any price." The following day or perhaps even some hours later, when Mark had calmed down, he would completely deny that the conversation had taken place and that particular opinion had been voiced.

Mark was either in total denial that he had made the statement, or felt foolish that he had caused such a severe argument to occur on an issue that was not only inconsequential, but total rubbish. Mark was always blameless and was cunning in shifting the blame of the argument to Nora. Her self-belief was low and, as a result of this, she was totally convinced that Mark was always right. This continued behavior on the part of Mark led Nora into thinking and, temporarily, believing that she was losing her mind. Nora ended up not knowing if, when Mark said something, he actually meant it. She was totally confused.

3. A very tearful lady confided that she had felt forced to ask her daughter (16 years of age) to leave the family home due to an ultimatum issued by her husband. The 16-year-old had deliberately driven her mum's car, as a learner driver, and crashed it. The damage had been repaired and paid for by the young girl, but still the incident caused a furious reaction from her stepfather. There was no discussion (I am told there never was) just a statement from him, prior to him storming off in his car, saying "That girl had better not be here when I return."

My patient was frightened, scared, devastated; she didn't know what to do or where to turn. She eventually decided to confide in the mum of her daughter's best friend who, kindly, came to the rescue and offered to have the daughter live with them. When my patient's husband returned to the home later that evening, he was very angry with his wife and blamed her for making the arrangements for the young girl to be re-housed elsewhere. He then proceeded to demand the return of 16 -year-old as soon as possible.

Negative responses on how to deal with someone who shifts blame:

- Agree with them that you are to blame and accept it

- Apologize, grovel, saying you are sorry repeatedly until you are forgiven

- Enter into lengthy, reasonable explanations as to why you are not to blame (this is usually a waste of time as they don't listen)

Positive responses on how to deal with someone who shifts blame

- Stand up for yourself. (This needn't be done aggressively)

- Continue to stand up for yourself on each occasion that arguments occur (again, do so non-aggressively). The saying 'gently, gently, catchy monkey' springs to mind

- Decide on a course of action that you feel is fair and acceptable to both of you

- Remind yourself that you are dealing with a naughty child (there is a child in all of us and when the child misbehaves this knowledge, when brought to the forefront of your mind, will sometimes help with the way you re-act to situations)

- Reject the blame—emotionally—blame is a burden and is negative energy

- Know you are right (does it matter what they believe?)

- It is not your responsibility to explain, at length, every issue that is discussed—don't do this—as this response repeated, on a regular basis, will drain and deflate you. It also absolves the other person of responsibility and accountability

- Not react to any verbal attack

- Divert the attack by introducing a different issue/topic (a temporary solution to an onslaught)

- Be as manipulative and cunning as the other person and, while acknowledging their opinion, not openly agree with them, but remove yourself from the situation and tell them that you need time to think things through.

> "All men and women have an equal need for love. When these needs are not fulfilled it is easy to have our feelings hurt, for which we blame our partner."
>
> —John Gray

Showing Disrespect

Showing disrespect demonstrates to someone that you don't love or like them. It is the ultimate nail in the coffin of a healthy relationship. There is no future if a partnership has no mutual respect. Respect is being civil and courteous and accepting that we are all different. Respect is being able to listen to what someone has to say without responding by ridiculing and hurting them. It is treating others as you would want to be treated yourself.

Examples of Disrespect

My client Joan told me of the episode that had finally ended all attempts at reconciling after a separation. Although her husband had moved to a different town, he came and stayed with her regularly and gave every indication that the relationship between them was "back on track".

A woman phoned him during one of his visits, and when the wife objected, he said that it was his right to speak to anyone he wanted to speak to, whether it be at his wife's house or anywhere else. He did not see that he was disrespecting his wife's hospitality, or destroying his attempts at getting back with her. It eventually emerged that he had been seeing this "other woman" behind his wife's back for quite some time and that she was pursuing him and quite prepared to break up a marriage in order to get her man.

Another patient told me how, if she displeased her husband, he felt he had to pay her back by turning his back on her all evening when in a pub having a drink. This behavior continued until she groveled and coaxed him back into a good humor.

You are being disrespectful if...

- You don't allow your partner space
- You fail to acknowledge your partner's input
- You don't allow your partner to share their worries
- You take complete control of your joint lives together (financially, emotionally, physically or spiritually)
- You deliberately hurt your partner
- You are undermining your partner
- You are intimidating your partner

- You are interrogating your partner
- Not giving positive criticism
- Being inflexible
- Being uncompassionate
- Always expecting your own way
- You use insults and bullying to make your partner surrender.
- You are being cunning and sly in order to get your own way.

Negative responses in dealing with disrespect

- Accept being overruled
- Accept always that you are wrong in your thinking and responses
- Bow to the superior knowledge of your persecutor
- Accept you are unworthy, useless and incapable in all areas
- Accept you will not amount to anything
- Accept that you are nothing without your partner

Positive responses on how to deal with disrespect:

- Realize and understand that disrespect for others comes from lack of self-respect
- Stand up for yourself
- Love yourself—no matter what
- Learn to respect yourself
- Put your own needs on the same level as that of other people
- Value yourself

- Appreciate who and what you are
- Acknowledge your experience and wisdom and act on it
- Don't react to unpleasant/inappropriate behavior—just be still within
- Realize that you don't have to react
- Remember that the little things don't matter
- Concern yourself with the bigger picture
- Create a life for yourself (with or without your partner)

> Throughout life people will make you mad, disrespect you and treat you badly. Let God deal with the things they do, 'cause hate in your heart will consume you too.
>
> —Will Smith

Criticism

The dictionary definition of a critic is:

"One who expresses a reasoned opinion on any matter especially involving a judgment of its value, truth, righteousness, beauty or technique. One who engages, often professionally, in the analysis, evaluation or appreciation of works of art or performance. One given to harsh or captious judgment." *Merriam-Webster*

We are all critics. Criticism is an observation.

To be constantly criticized is to be constantly undermined. Criticism is a powerful tool, which, used consistently, will create a dependent, powerless, unconfident person who is unable to function alone. It takes away an individual's identity and ability to think or act alone. It is the start of a process of depersonalization. The ultimate aim of criticism is to control.

Here are some examples of criticism:

- A patient said that her husband apologized to people they were both in conversation with if, in his opinion, his wife said something that he did not agree with. This made her feel vulnerable and inadequate and this action stopped her from taking part in conversations when he was present. He made remarks, such as, "Don't mind my wife, she doesn't understand what we are talking about." In the early days of their relationship, she confronted him regarding this only to be told that "It was a joke, and you're taking it too seriously." Some joke eh? At her expense. Making fun of someone else in a derogatory way is to criticize and undermine that person.

- Having the dishes examined after you have washed and dried them.

- When doing the laundry, Jane said that if one of the items fell to the ground during the process of hanging the items on the washing line, her husband would be dissatisfied with the garment's cleanliness and would make her wash the item again.

- Being told you cannot accomplish or reach a target as efficiently as your partner, from filling in crossword puzzles to furthering your career.

- Being told, repeatedly, that "you are nothing without me."

Negative criticism:

Is how we respond when we want to undermine another person in order to

- Get our own way

- Feel superior
- Feel in control
- Apportion blame
- Make someone feel unconfident
- Make someone feel worthless
- Make someone feel unloved
- Make someone feel unwanted
- Make someone feel insecure

Positive criticism

Is how we respond when we want to assist someone:
- To enable
- To understand
- To assist
- To support
- To share
- To develop
- To evaluate
- To give confidence
- To make someone feel valued
- To make someone feel worthy
- To make someone feel secure
- To make someone feel loved.

Negative responses to criticism:

- Swallow the criticism and allow the critic to make you feel bad
- Feel vulnerable and weak

- Give up
- Say you will never do it again (whatever it is)
- Feel insecure and unloved
- Feel worthless
- Allow it to affect your life

Positive responses to negative criticism:

- Say thank you and ignore it
- Take it with a pinch of salt
- Realize who and where it's coming from and accept its source as clouded and unacceptable
- Learn to detach from negative people who are controllers
- Get constructive and valuable criticism from people you know love, respect and support you.

> "We cannot achieve more in life than what we believe in our heart of hearts we deserve to have."
> —James R. Ball

Intimidation

This behavior is activated in order to humiliate someone into submission (emotional or physical). It is always offensive, vindictive and cruel. It is a calculated way of controlling a person and/or situation. It is an abuse of power and authority. Continued use of intimidation can wear an individual down to such a degree that they become disempowered and emotionally disabled. They become "puppets" and can only do what they are told. This is mind-manipulation/mind control.

It is very powerful, and the victim usually discovers that they have been the subject of this control too late to turn the situation around easily. The situation can, of course, be stopped. However, when you are afraid of your controller and you have been on the receiving end of years of intimidation, your energy, motivation, and belief in your own power is low. This is the reason it is difficult to turn the situation around to your way.

Here are some examples of intimidation:

- Being shouted and/or sworn at
- Being constantly criticized
- The use of threatening body language targeted at you
- Being ignored
- Being blamed for another's actions
- Being told, repeatedly, that you are nothing on your own and that you need them as you are nothing without them.
- Being made wrong for everything you say or do.

Example of Intimidation

During a counseling session, a lady told me that she was afraid to go to sleep at night because her husband said that he was going to kill her and the children while she slept. She felt that this threat had been substantiated when she woke one night to find him lying at her side holding a mallet in his hand which hovered dangerously over her head. His eyes were glassy and crazed, and, with his face right up to hers, told her not to sleep or he would carry out his threats.

She told me that she knew, deep down, that he would not carry out the threat as he had never been physically violent in the relationship and he loved his children too much to ever do them any physical harm. She nevertheless was frightened and did as she was told.

Eventually, she was to find out that this situation came about because her husband was jealous of her. She was a friendly, humorous, outgoing and popular person with many friends and acquaintances. She was also devoted to her husband and her children and had never wanted to be with anyone else during the course of their marriage. She was unaware of his jealous nature and, therefore, could not understand his resulting behavior. When she asked him what had she done wrong and why he was behaving in this way, he always replied menacingly, "You know what you have done." She didn't. The threats and intimidation continued and the fear it provoked in her resulted in this couple divorcing. When you are constantly intimidated to this extent, you believe and are fearful that anything is possible.

> "I had my bully, and it was excruciating. Not only the bully, but the intimidation I felt."
> —Robert Cormier

Negative responses to intimidation:

- You become indecisive
- You become vulnerable
- You feel under stress
- You become isolated
- You will have poor concentration
- You will become anxious
- You will become depressed
- You might increase your use of alcohol, cigarettes, or drugs
- You might underperform at work
- You will become inarticulate
- You will have high blood pressure
- You will have sleepless nights

Positive responses on how to deal with intimidation:

- Realize what is happening and don't respond to the controller

- However tempted you are—don't react

- Change your response to the controller: Before entering into any discussion with the controller, mentally run over the conversation that is going to take place and change the sequence and patterns of what you always say. If you do this, it will put pressure on the other person to change their responses.

- Put a protective barrier around yourself—you can do this through meditation

- Keep a journal of your repeated arguments and write down the reservoir of responses available to you

- Attempt various responses and reactions (as above) the next time the argument takes place

- Share your feelings with a trusted friend/member of the family for support

- Seek Counseling (through your General Practitioner/Health Centre)

- Decide to do something for yourself (a new hobby, a regular evening out, etc) in order to raise your self-esteem and develop your confidence

- Learn a new skill through you local community college. This will enhance your self-image and offer you the opportunity of either becoming employed or getting a better job

- Acknowledge and value yourself and the skills and abilities you already have

- Write out a Mantra. This is a statement of what you want in, and from, your life. It need be no more than four lines. You can write anything you want. A good example is "I am as good as anyone else. I will improve, on a daily basis, to become emotionally and financially independent."

You become a victim when you sabotage yourself and/or your partner

People sabotage themselves in order to stay the same. They dare not take risks and change anything, because that would risk not being in control of their lives, homes and people. Saboteurs are also afraid of change. They stay the same to stay in control. The saboteur will be afraid of fundamental issues such as moving house, new job opportunities, new friends, new social habitats and new hobbies. These are all potential circumstances that would change the saboteur's life and might result in something being taken away from them.

The risk is too big, so they opt to stay in the cocoon of their own making. Unfortunately, when this happens, they usually take prisoners with them who are also trapped in their cocoon. This cocoon stops the people they are close to from progressing and moving forward in their lives.

Saboteurs are selfish and stuck in a rut of their own making. They cause the people who fall in love with them horrendous misery and unhappiness. Saboteurs firmly established within a family are reluctant and resistant to any change of circumstances. This is due to the saboteur's inflexibility and uncompromising attitude, and fear of losing this secure position in the family unit.

Rules are established in the household, imposed by the saboteur, and if these rules are broken, all hell breaks loose. These rules can be as inconsequential as always ensuring that doors are closed behind you if you leave a room, to never staying out later in the evening without prior permission from the saboteur. If these rules are broken, the consequences to the perpetrator are horrendous. Anger abounds in order to ensure that, in future, no rules are broken. I have heard patients who have, themselves, imposed these rules say that this is how to gain the respect they feel they deserve. Unfortunately, this is not so. This household is managed by fear and there is no respect.

Positive options to handle a relationship saboteur

- Ensure that the rules of the household are agreed by all who live in the house
- Ensure that the rules are realistic and appropriate
- Agree to allow some flexibility of the rules
- Agree that if a rule is broken, the issue will be discussed as a family unit and the person punished appropriately
- Agree that there will be a trial period for the imposed rules.

Examples of self-sabotage:

A man who saw me on a regular basis told me that he needed to earn more money in order to sustain the standard of living in the household. He was a successful, clever guy with many skills. Unfortunately, as he explained, his financial position had remained the same, and had not risen in line with the "extras" both he and his partner enjoyed. He explored avenues of making extra money, i.e., finding a new job, starting up his own business. All the avenues he explored offered opportunities. There was the possibility of starting up his own business (with a colleague), also, the opportunity of working in another country (for a limited period) with the prospect of excellent financial payoffs.

However, after lengthy discussions with his partner he opted to remain doing the same job he had always done for the same financial return. This resulted in the family lowering their standard of living to accommodate this decision. Ultimately he was afraid of taking a risk and changing his professional working pattern. He gave up and gave in. As a consequence to this decision, over a period of time, he became lethargic, unmotivated and lacking in self-respect.

Another example:

One young girl came to see me at the Health Centre. She was very pretty, talented and articulate. However, she believed she was unattractive and useless. She repeatedly told herself, when looking in the mirror, how ugly she was and asked why would anyone want to be with her? The same pattern occurred before every job interview she attended. She asked herself, "Why would they hire me of all people?" This young lady was brainwashing herself into believing that nothing good was going to come her way. She was sabotaging herself. "If you believe you can't—you won't."

How to Deal With a Self-Saboteur

Here are some examples of negative responses:

- Listen to the saboteur's plans and take them with a "pinch of salt".

- Don't believe everything they tell you

- Don't rely on the outcome they expect

- Always have a realistic Plan B (one that involves you.)

- While being flexible and adaptable—don't be fooled into believing everything is going to be alright because the saboteur said so

- If there is something you want (i.e., buy a house, buy a car, getting a job, changing the kids' school), make sure that you research the commodity, discuss and prepare all documentation thoroughly with professionals prior to presenting it to your partner. Introduce the subject gently and informally at first (getting them used to the idea). They will initially resist taking the risk. However, gentle persuasion and negotiating skills will win with perseverance.

Positive points:

- Give the saboteur encouragement and support whenever possible

- Reinforce the saboteur's good points

- Try to keep the saboteur within realistic boundaries of their expectations of themselves

- When discussions arise, paraphrase (so that the saboteur can see that you understand the topic being discussed). Offer logical responses giving examples of the points you identify. This helps to reinforce, clarify and justify your conclusions, thereby allowing no error for misconception of your opinions

- Encourage this individual to set themselves small achievable targets and support them in obtaining a positive result

- Create your own security blanket. Give yourself rewards, treats

- Learn to be self-sufficient

- Tackle the obstacles that you have been scared of—trust me, they will become easier.

- Learn to handle your own finances

- Be safe in the knowledge that the people you both come into contact with are aware of your circumstances and secretly support you.

> "You are what you think. You are what you go for. You are what you do!"   —Bob Richards

3   How Do You Become a Victim?

People become victims for different reasons. First of all, let us look at the thinking and behavior that identifies you as a victim.

Ask yourself these questions.

- Do you feel able to discuss issues in your relationship with your partner?
- Does your partner ridicule you, humiliate you?
- Does your partner 'play up' if you are invited out with friends?
- Does your partner hold the financial purse strings in your relationship?
- Do you tend to agree with your partner rather than face the aggressive outcome if you do not?
- Does your happiness in your relationship depend on your partner's mood?
- Do you feel trapped in your relationship?
- Do you think that you should stay in the relationship because you believe you cannot cope alone?
- Are you afraid of your partner?

Everyone's list will be different. Make your own list in order to decide if you are a victim, or living with a victim. Most women believe that if they are not physically damaged by their partner, that they are not being abused in their relationship. This is not true. If you are being ignored, humiliated, undermined, drained of energy and railroaded in your relationship, then you are being abused. In fact, emotional abuse can be more damaging than physical abuse.

Emotional abuse can rob you of your identity, personality and characteristics. You will become a brainwashed robot that does your partner's bidding. A controlling partner will use brainwashing to gain control in the relationship. Brainwashing is used to railroad a partner into submission. When you are the subject of being brainwashed, you will be unaware that this is taking place, because it is a slow deliberate method of taking power away from you and in doing so will strengthen your partner.

Here are some examples of what continued brainwashing can achieve:

- Rob you of personal power and energy
- Results in you being emotionally disabled and reliant on your partner
- Keeps you in ignorance of what is actually going on, and the changes taking place in your relationship
- Isolates you from family and friends
- Denies you control of your finances
- Changes who you are and what you think
- Makes you powerless
- Destroys your self-esteem and confidence

You will become a victim as a result of your early learning experiences from your role models (parents/grandparents/aunts/uncles, etc.). If you have seen your mother/father behaving as a victim you will have learned that this is the way to react. This way of interacting will form your repeating pattern in adult life.

Here are some examples of how you become a victim:

- If a parent constantly put you down
- If a parent called you names

- If a parent threatened and/or frightened you

- If a parent bought your silence (bribery)

- If a parent put the fear of God into you

- By complying with your partner's demands and wanting to have peace at any price

- By believing that you are always wrong

- By believing that you are guilty

- If you have a low self-esteem, no confidence and are afraid to make decisions

- If you are threatened physically and/or emotionally

- By depending on someone else/your partner to sort things out for you. This is an avoidance strategy. This form of response can arise through learned behavior (if you ask your partner to do something for you and they comply you might do this repeatedly in order to avoid taking action yourself)

- By deliberately putting yourself down (this is usually done to give your partner some cadence and authority over you. Although this may work in the short term, in the long-term you will suffer from your own action)

- The victim will be at their partner's mercy

- The victim will smile when they want to cry

- The victim will pretend that everything is all right

- The victim will tip-toe around their partner all the time (treading on egg shells)

- The victim will do their partner's bidding—no matter the consequences to yourself

- The victim will give up on themselves

- The victim will experience suppressed anger and frustration

- The victim will become non-descript
- The victim will have a low self-esteem
- The victim will block out emotions
- The victim will believe they are unloved
- The victim will live their life flat-lining

Rewards for Being a Victim

Here are some examples of the rewards:
- You get sympathy
- You get cared for
- You get lots of attention
- You are made to feel special
- You feel secure
- You feel safe
- You avoid everything and can justify doing so
- You are in control, albeit negative control
- You are not accountable
- You are not responsible
- You cannot be blamed when things go wrong

Parental Behavior

Your role models are the people you learn from on how to think, behave and communicate in families. Parents do the best job they can and should not be blamed for the way you have been raised. You are now an adult and can choose to behave in a different way.

Here are examples of tactics used by a bad father:
- 'Buying' the children with presents, days out, etc.

- Putting their mom, his wife, down in front of the children, often using humor
- Calling their mom names in front of the children
- Asking the children to check up on their mom
- Treating his wife, their mom, badly and using her as a servant to meet his needs
- Threats of severe punishment should the children make mistakes
- Bullying the children
- Being moody and withdrawn
- Expecting to be the master of the house
- Being unsupportive to his wife
- Doing nothing around the house
- High expectations of his children
- Provides no stability for the family
- Expecting the rest of the household to 'tread on eggshells' around him in order to keep him in a good mood
- Is violent in front of the children
- Doesn't care that he is a bad role model
- Is not responsible for providing financial security (spends money as fast as he earns it)
- Discourages friends of the children coming to the house by embarrassing his own children and other children

Here are some examples of tactics used by a good father:
- Does his share of the household tasks
- Is prepared to change nappies, or get up in the night to feed the baby

- Supports his wife/partner's decisions
- Shares financial responsibility
- Treats the children with respect
- Does his share of child minding
- Plays with the children
- Encourages the children to bring their friends home
- Believes that daughters are as valuable as sons
- Believes that children should not be exposed to violence in the home
- Believes that fathers should be good role models and should behave well

It is not just men that are bad influences and role models. Women have their part to play and the above list can also apply to women. Make your own list of the experiences you have encountered. The list will be different for each on of us.

Are you really a victim?

A more focused way of interpreting the word "victim" is to understand that a victim accepts the name and becomes a target. If you accept that you are a target in your relationship, you will accept all the crap thrown at you. You can decide at any time not to be a target and instead become an independent empowered individual. If you have been hurt by someone playing mind games with you, or if you are the target of someone's anger, decide to stop this NOW.

Stop yourself from being a target, change the thought of being a target and replace the word with another more appropriate and positive one: that of a 'survivor'. Remember you are what you think you are. So, if you see yourself as a victim that is exactly what you will be. Thoughts are very powerful so change the negative victim thought into a positive survivor thought. When you decide to become a survivor, the word will have a strong impact in the way you perceive yourself and how others perceive you.

Here are some examples of how you and others will see that you are no longer a victim:

- You will not allow anyone to abuse you either emotionally or physically anymore
- You will attract friends who are also survivors and positive people
- You will look after yourself and no longer suffer accusations/ridicule from your partner or anyone else
- You will expect equality in a relationship
- You will regain your self-respect
- You will regain your confidence
- You will become empowered
- You will have energy
- You will stop kidding yourself that your relationship is good
- You will feel more secure in your relationship because you are in control of yourself
- You will face fear and confrontation and believe in who you are and what you say
- You will not need rescuing from the normal everyday tasks that you have not taken responsibility for up to this point

I am sure that you can think of many more examples pertinent to your circumstances.

> "Sympathy for victims is always counter-balanced by an equal and opposite feeling of resentment towards them."
>
> Ben Elton

4 | Do You Want to Change?

To change from being a victim to becoming a survivor requires strength of mind, determination and focus. Changing a repeating pattern is difficult. It can be done, but will only be done successfully with constant practice.

Why Do You Want to Become a Survivor?

Here are some examples to help you:

- to have a better life
- to lift your self-esteem
- to overcome fears
- to regain your confidence
- to let go of past hurts
- to move on in your life
- to take responsibility for yourself
- to fulfill your dreams
- to be a better parent
- to set a good example for your children
- because you don't want to rely on your partner/family/friends anymore
- to feel good about yourself
- to further develop yourself
- to enjoy an equal, loving relationship with your partner. "

There are advantages to be gained from your past difficult experiences. Having worked through the strategy I am outlining in this book, you can make your difficult experiences work for you. When you are able to turn your negative experiences into positive action, you will have accepted and confronted the emotional upsets, fear and pain you have gone through and have survived. In activating this process, you will have the skill to support others to follow the same road to recovery.

On the road from victim to survivor, it will be necessary to face your demons and overcome your issues. How do you know you have successfully completed the process?

Indicators of Change: Victim to Survivor

- You will have a greater understanding of how your thoughts can influence your feelings and behavior
- You will not be afraid to discuss your fears
- You will have learned how to relax (meditation/writing in your journal/walking the dog, etc)
- You will have learned to trust your partner/family/friends
- You will know where to get support and how to give support yourself
- You will have learned self discipline
- You will know the difference between pertinent and impertinent in conversations with you partner/family/friends
- You will enjoy taking responsibility for yourself
- You will value yourself
- You will be able to communicate your thoughts and feelings to your partner

- You will enjoy being the new you and will have accepted the change that has taken place

The above are examples of some of the benefits that you will experience through the changing process. Your list will be different.

> "We cannot live the afternoon of life according to the program of life's morning; for what in the morning was true will in evening become a lie."
>
> -- C.G. Jung

Relationship Development

In order to have a fulfilling intimate relationship, it is important that both people in the relationship are allowed to grow independently as well as together. Your personal growth is your own responsibility and cannot be foisted upon another. Growing as an individual should not have a negative impact on your intimate relationship with your partner. If one partner resents and stops the other from developing as an individual, the relationship will inevitably falter because the foundation of the relationship is not being nourished through new experiences.

In order for a relationship to have positive growth, it requires freedom, respect, and love. A positive intimate relationship should forge new ground and not be stuck in time. There should be no restrictions in the relationship other than the boundaries that both partners have agreed to at the onset. Naturally there will be changes as children grow up or aging relatives need care, etc.

As you care for yourself, so should you care for your partner. It is for this reason that it is important to love yourself first. That might be an unpopular concept, but I believe that your first commitment is to yourself. The passion with which you love yourself and are true to yourself will have a positive effect on your partner, family and friends.

Loving yourself is a difficult thing to do. None of us are perfect. We all have imperfections. Loving yourself, warts and all, is to be self-aware and unafraid to acknowledge your imperfections. Loving yourself is making a non-verbal agreement with yourself to continue addressing these imperfections as best as you can. If you stay aware of your imperfections, you will be able to communicate and interact with your partner and others being mindful and cautious at all times of your own limitations, baggage and hang-ups.

Learning not to react spontaneously during discussions with your partner will help you to understand your own misunderstanding of any issue raised. Everybody enters into relationships with expectations and baggage. You start off thinking that you know what you need from your relationship. However, it is often the case that when you identify that you are not getting what you need from your relationship, it will start spinning downwards toward separation and divorce.

In order to get what you need and want from a relationship, you have to be realistic and communicate to your partner the catalog of needs and wants you expect. Both partners should identify their expectations from the other. Honest communication is vital so that you both completely understand the other's needs. Communicating your expectations will give each partner the opportunity to face the needs and wants of the other and will simplify the process of establishing aims and objectives for the partnership. Both of you can choose who, what and how you will be each day.

If you want to change your relationship, you must change yourself first. In order to change your thinking and behavior, you must first of all face the demons that you must release to break the chains of your old negative, destructive patterns of thought. Remember, you are in control of yourself. No one else controls you. Your partner can only control you with your permission. When you are successful at changing yourself, your relationship will change as a result.

Commitment

Commitment is to give a firm promise that can be relied upon. When you make a commitment to your partner, what you are saying is that you are aiming for the best possible outcome for both of you. This commitment involves sharing, caring and growth both independently and together in your relationship. One school of thought states that all relationships have a beginning, a middle path of growth and an end of the journey. In order to fully live in the moment and experience passion in your relationship, you must open your heart to your partner without feeling afraid of doing so. One of the aims of a commitment between two people should be for each of you to grow individually and to grow together.

Both of you should acknowledge and accept that each of you will change as you develop individually and this change will result in a change in your relationship. Being aware of constant change in each other, and in your relationship, will act as a safety net for the both of you. Changing independently and together can be risky as you plough into the unknown. However, the plus side is a positive possibility of having a lasting, loving, growing relationship that is more fulfilling and passionate. All positive relationships grow through changing to meet both partners' needs, wants and desires. Honest continued commitment is built though this changing process.

> Don't smother each other. No one can grow in the shade.
> —Leo Buscaglia

Ask yourself, "What do I need from my relationship?"

Here are some examples to help you in this process:

- I need to trust my partner
- I need to feel loved
- I need to be able to communicate with my partner

- I need to have faith that my partner will be loyal, faithful and committed

- I need to have an equal say in my relationship with my partner

- I need to respect my partner

- I need to know that my partner will stand by me whatever the circumstances

These are only some of the needs. Write your own needs down so that you can be clear about what it is you need from your part.

> "Oh, the comfort—the inexpressible comfort of feeling *safe* with a person—having neither to weigh thoughts nor measure words, but pouring them all right out, just as they are, chaff and grain together; certain that a faithful hand will take and sift them, keep what is worth keeping, and then with the breath of kindness blow the rest away."
> ~Dinah Craik, *A Life for a Life*, 1859

| 5 | **The Process of Change** |

To change your repeating pattern is to take responsibility for your thoughts and behavior. As a result of this action, you will change the way your partner and others perceive you. The negative repeating pattern you have brought with you into adulthood is responsible for who and what you have become. I believe it is pointless to blame your parents or other early role models for your behavior as an adult. It is too easy to blame your thinking, behavior and circumstances on your past experiences. Instead, when you identify that your reactions to a set of circumstances in the here and now are inappropriate, the adult reaction is to change that pattern from a negative to positive. Everyone has a belief system and your positive belief system should include that:

- You have the right to speak up for yourself

- You have the right to an opinion

- You have a right to be heard.

> "The measure of success is not whether you have a tough problem to deal with, but whether it's the same problem you had last year."
> -- John Foster Dulles

Don't React

Don't fall into the trap of always responding and reacting to your partner immediately. If you are a victim and living with a controller, you will want to respond immediately to questions posed to you because you want to stay on the right side of your partner. The single most powerful lesson I have learned is to be still in the mind and shut up.

The first step, in my experience is not to *react* so eagerly to every situation, sentence, nuance or facial expression. This is challenging if you are a reactive person. You must be determined, however, to try your best and see what happens. Keep yourself focused on your decision and deliberately stop yourself reacting by:

- Diverting the conversation

- Leaving the room on some pretence—just to engineer time to think of an appropriate response or, indeed, no response at all.

You will be amazed at the difference in the dynamics of the household. Peace reigns for quite some considerable time. When asked a question, sometimes you can pretend you don't know the answer and wait until the person involved comes to their own conclusion. The waiting is frustrating at first, but eventually you will enjoy the fact that the pressure is off you to always have the answers, or find solutions.

There are little tricks you can adopt along the way. For example, if asked a question you don't want to answer, look directly at someone else. When you do this, the focus goes off you and transfers to the other person to do the answering. Believe me, this works. I have used this in professional situations also. If you don't know the answer, or the answer you want to give is too contentious, look at someone else and they automatically take the lead in answering the question. Try it. Try to keep this non-reaction up—that's all you do.

The most common mistake we make in trying to change patterns within ourselves is to do too much too soon. Just take that one simple step and continue doing it for a few months. Don't be tempted to bring anything else into the equation. Lie fallow. Rest your mind during this time and watch others around you changing the way they handle situations without you being involved in the decision process. This simple adjustment has many benefits.

Remember:

- You don't have to say what you feel
- You don't have to agree with your partner through fear
- You don't have to solve your partner's problems
- You don't have to express your opinion
- You can't be blamed if things go wrong
- You can maintain your energy
- Become an observer rather than a participator
- You are not responsible for the outcome
- You won't be seen as a know-it-all
- You become surprised at the way others think and solve their differences without your intervention
- You allow others to grow up
- You allow others to take responsibility for their behavior, speech, actions
- You observe the development of ideas and thoughts around you
- You see you are not needed to solve everything
- You are not the baddy anymore

These are just a few of the points you will observe when using this process. It is empowering and you will relax into your new strategy.

What if this is as good as it gets?

You may recognize the phrase *As Good as It Gets*. It is the 1997 film starring Jack Nicholson and Helen Hunt—an Academy Award Winner. When I saw the film and heard that particular line, it struck a chord in me. I applied the line to my own life. What if this is as good as it gets? A sobering thought if life hasn't turned out the way you had hoped it would.

Everyone has preconceived ideas of what they expect from life. Your expectations are usually full of perfect scenarios, a variety of exciting experiences that all have satisfactory outcomes. In your mind, your futures should end up "happy ever after." Look around: how many people do you know who live "happily ever after" lives? I can't think of any.

Everybody compromises by being adaptable in order to blend in and put up with stuff they don't necessarily agree with. Everyone faces problems and difficulties at some stage, on all levels of life, be it personally or professionally. Some are better at hiding it than others. Some are better at coping with their particular circumstances. But everyone has their share of personal problems.

- Have you ever thought that somebody else is leading the life you'd love?

- Have you ever said to yourself, "I'll have whatever they are ordering?"

Life is difficult. Never were truer words written. Life for us all is difficult. Take a look at your own life—what if this is as good as your life is going to get? Are you happy with it? Are you satisfied with your lot?

If not, then perhaps this book will help turn your life around by looking at yourself and changing negative, inappropriate patterns of behavior you have been repeating all your life. In order to live the life you want, you have to reinvent it. You can do this. You have the power to transform your life.

- Changing yourself it will allow you to be who you want to be

- Changing yourself it will alter your outlook on yourself and others

- You will change your partner's behavior by changing yours

- Changing yourself is the key to all change

The mind has two major parts: the conscious and the unconscious. The conscious mind is the bit we use to think through a problem.

The unconscious is where our feelings, beliefs and memories live, and this part of our brain does not use logic—it "thinks" symbolically. And the unconscious is much the bigger part. For example,

- You eat too much because you enjoy it even though you know it's bad for you

- You don't do the work you should because there's something else you enjoy, and prefer to do

- You want the new job and the extra money, but you don't believe you are ready for the responsibility

- There is a logical reason for doing something—but you don't believe you can do it and can't be bothered to try.

What you think determines how you feel. Understanding this connection will be central to your success at changing yourself. The basic truth is that your feelings, good or bad, are the product of your own thoughts. You have to think about something before you feel it.

> Whether you think you can or think you can't, you are right.
>
> —Henry Ford

You can't make positive changes in lifelong patterns if you think of yourself as powerless. This thought will totally disable you. If you see yourself as powerless, you deny yourself the enjoyment of the power that is rightfully yours. If you think you don't have power in the situation you are in, try this exercise:

"What are three ways in which I could make my situation worse?" If you can answer this question, and I am sure that you can, then maybe there are three ways in which you can make it better.

In order to empower yourself, you need to understand your thinking, and your beliefs have to be clear and positive. Effort and struggle are all signs that you are fighting with yourself—that you are at cross purposes with your own deeply held belief system.

Your mind is the control center of your behavior and your behavior is what determines who you are and what you accomplish.

The first thing to do if you decide you want to change your patterns of behavior is to:

- Take responsibility for where you are now.

- Don't blame yourself for everything that's gone wrong in your life. Indulging in this thought process can only lead to feelings of regret and "if only." These thoughts will leave you negative and lacking in energy. You need your batteries charged and filled with energy to change yourself.

Don't Expect Anything from Anyone Else

You will only be disappointed if you have expectations of others. You are always ready to blame others for not making you happy, for not giving you the love you want, for not providing you with a comfortable existence.

I have come across many people who have relied on their partner for happiness. They have placed the responsibility for their happiness and future comforts on someone else. They have put another person under considerable pressure (albeit unintentionally) to give them what they want. Most people do this because they don't believe they could do all these things for themselves.

Some people are brainwashed into believing that they are incapable of accomplishing anything for themselves. They lack self-worth or self-confidence. They have no faith in their ability to give themselves what they want. So they accept these labels that are placed on them and feel overwhelming gratitude that they have a good life through someone else's efforts and endeavors. They don't see during the time this is happening that the perception they had of themselves was due to a master stroke of someone else having total control of them and their life.

You must all think for yourselves and not put the responsibility for your happiness on another person. **"If it's going to be, it's up to me."**

Here is an example of a repeating pattern:

A lady I counseled told me that whenever she and her husband were watching a film on the television, her husband would asked her the name of the leading actor. She would respond by providing him with the name and also gave him an account of the actor's career including titles of other films he/she had starred in. By the time she had finished this monologue, she had lost the storyline of the film and would go to the kitchen to make a coffee for them. On returning to the living room with the coffee, she always found that her husband had switched channels and was watching something he enjoyed.

This scenario was replayed over and over for some ten years before she discovered that this was one of her husband's strategies to take her attention from something she was enjoying by engaging her in a game that she couldn't resist, imparting all the information she could muster to answer his question. Her husband wasn't really interested in the actor or the film but he knew that she couldn't resist spouting forth her knowledge on the subject. This situation kept repeating so that he could have the channel on the television that interested him. He knew that if he asked her a question, her answer would be so thorough that her concentration on the film would be distracted and he would have his own way watching what he wanted to see. A subtle and unobtrusive method of getting your own way. When she eventually realized what was happening, she changed her game to counteract his strategy:

She altered the scenario, so when they were both watching a film on the television and he asked, "Who is that actor?" her changed response was, "I don't know. Who do you think the actor/actress is?" She simply carried on watching the film. She knew the answer to the question, of course. More importantly he knew that she knew the answer to the question. But now that she had cottoned on to his game, she blocked his move and was able to continue watching the film.

She has reached the conclusion that she doesn't care if her husband doesn't know the name of the actor. She has relinquished her negative control of giving out superfluous information. She doesn't see it as necessary anymore to impart her knowledge to uninterested parties. If her husband really wants to know the answer to any question he asks her, he can look online to find it. She believed for years that it was part of her role in the relationship to make things better for her partner, whatever the issue.

> "If you can dream, it you can do it"
> —Walt Disney

<table>
<tr><td>

6

</td><td>

Being Realistic

</td></tr>
</table>

Stay in the Here and Now

When situations arise that spiral out of control, stay in reality. See it for what it is. Remember other situations that were similar, and ask yourself the following questions:

- How did these start?
- Where did they lead on to?
- What happened?
- What was the outcome?

Remember, it is important that you stay in control of your emotions. Don't let your partner override your control by bullying you, intimidating or interrogating you. Stay in reality. Think about what they actually want from the process they are engaging you in. If you think carefully and objectively, you will know the underlying problem and the anticipated outcome. Take stock, don't panic. Instead of panicking, think the situation through. Above all, else don't react.

Being realistic when you are faced with an emotional problem is the hardest thing to achieve because you are involved in the emotion.

Here are some examples of what you can do in this situation:

- Stand back from the issue and stay outside the problem (so that you can interpret the problem objectively)
- Think of how you believe your partner might want you to react on this issue
- Ask yourself what reward your partner gets if you react the same way as you always have reacted?

- If you are being pressured to react, do so by saying that you need more time to think through the issues your partner is raising.

Being realistic and keeping a clear head could result in the situation resolving itself. Being realistic has benefits! Here are some examples:

- You stay in the here and now
- You give yourself time to unravel your fears, thoughts, actions
- You allow others to think things through on their own
- You allow time for people to come to their own conclusions
- You don't act in a panic
- You find out what you want to achieve
- You find out the outcome the others want to achieve
- You re-assess your principles, values, beliefs
- You let the dust settle
- You give yourself time to just be

Staying in Reality

- is accepting yourself for who you are.
- is accepting your childhood experiences and leaving them behind.
- is living in the here and now.
- is knowing where you are heading (aims and objectives).
- is knowing your partner's faults and finding the best option for dealing with every situation that presents itself.

> If you don't change, reality in the end forces that change upon you.
>
> Stuart Wilde

Staying in Reality has many benefits. When I was counseling in the primary healthcare setting, I helped many women whose husband's had left them after their children had grown up and moved out. When this happens and the husband leaves after many years of marriage, the wife is stunned and stupefied and believes the only reason her husband has left is because he has found a younger model. I believe that this is an easy "get out" answer for the wife to accept rather than looking closer at the real reason the marriage has failed.

All of the women I counseled in this scenario had essentially "given up" in their marriages. They all had felt safe and secure and did nothing to reestablish any form of intimacy. Kissing, touching, and sexual intercourse no longer interested them and they alone had decided enough was enough. They didn't want an intimate relationship anymore, so they put the brakes on and stopped it happening.

More than that, all the women I counseled had put on an enormous amount of weight during the course of their marriage and dressed in outdated, unfashionable clothes. I am not suggesting that attractive clothes and a slim body should necessarily be mandatory for a close relationship. I am, however, saying that no-one should feel secure and safe and especially so when they make no effort to keep their man. It is an act of utter complacency to believe that no one else wants your man and any woman who believes this is a fool.

The fact is that men who leave their wives after many years of marriage are searching for a loving, interesting, caring, loving partner and if this person happens to be younger—so be it. Women of a certain age (and I am one of them) should understand that if they say "no" to sex with their partner, this does not mean that their partner accepts this new rule. When I have raised this issue with men who left their wives after years of marriage, all agreed that they had become disenchanted with the marriage many years before they had left and had only stayed until the children became self-sufficient.

When people are having trouble with their marriage, it is because they are expecting it to run on automatic pilot. They think it will hang together through no effort of their own; unfortunately, it won't. Your relationship has to be worked on constantly.

Staying Focused

Life is full of ways to become distracted. Here are some examples of how to stay focused:

- Keep your reason for staying focused in the forefront of your mind.

- "The road to hell is paved with good intentions" is an old saying. You can have all the best intentions in the world, but if you don't see them through, they are worthless

- Be motivated. Stay firm. Discipline yourself

- Switch your mind from the negative thought you have previously focused on to a positive thought

- Don't listen to anyone else's advice. Nothing must put you off.

- Don't let your family and friends run over you

- Allow some time for yourself each day. Let your body and brain relax 10—30 minutes each day. Some people meditate, some look out of the window, others just close their eyes and relax. This time spent quietly will help you gain a clearer picture of what you want to achieve and you may find that you have solved some of the problems you didn't have answers for by just being still

- Take care of yourself and build your energy. You can't concentrate if you are too tired, too lonely, too hungry, too thirsty, etc.

- When too many things compete for your attention, order them according to urgency, and deal with them one at a time.

- Self-observation such as keeping a notebook is an alternative to seeking out others. It offers some of the same benefits, including venting of feelings, distancing yourself from the situation, and increased perspective of your goals. List your priorities. During the day, jot down anything that comes into your mind. Organize your thoughts in this way. Doing this will free up the chaos your brain experiences when there's a lot on your mind. This simple task allows you to concentrate on one thing at a time, Keep the notebook with you at all times

- Remember, making changes in the way we think takes time and effort—don't give up

> Only when your consciousness is totally focused on the moment you are in can you receive whatever gift, lesson, or delight that moment has to offer.
> —Barbara de Angelis

Being realistic is to have realistic goals and expectations. If your joint goals are different and unrealistic, then neither of you will be able to reach them.

Relationship goals

A goal is:
- Something to be aimed for by both partners in a relationship
- Time-limited

- Realistic and achievable
- Agreed to by each partner
- Flexible, allowing time for set-backs
- Mutually beneficial
- An objective that reflects the individual needs of each partner
- Something that fulfills the needs, wants and desires of both partners

How to achieve goals

- By supporting each other
- By having open, honest communication with each other
- By helping each other to grow as individuals
- By being aware of possible set-backs
- By respecting each other
- By introducing problem solving techniques to address conflicts when they arise
- By being non-judgmental of each other
- By being non critical of each other
- By giving each other space to develop
- By staying in the moment and enjoying each other.

> To climb steep hills requires slow pace at first
> —William Shakespeare, *Henry VIII, Act I*

7 Devise a Long-Term Strategy

What is a strategy? A strategy is a plan. A satisfactory, enjoyable life does not happen by accident. It has to be planned just as you would plan a good, rewarding, restful, holiday.

Ask yourself the following questions:

- **What** do you want out of life?

- **What** do you want in your life?

- **What** are you prepared to do to get it?

- **What** do you **need** to do to get what you want?

The first key in devising a long-term strategy is to take personal responsibility for the choices you have made so far in your life. Take no blame for this. You are where you are and that cannot be changed. Don't carry the baggage of wrong decisions because that will hold you back from achieving your objective.

To keep moving forward, you must focus on the future and on making your life the way you want it to be. Don't sit back and remain a victim waiting for good things to happen. They won't.

Practical and Emotional Blocks

The second key is to recognize the blocks in our life. Blocks are things that "get on your nerves." While some of these blocks appear small and insignificant, taken together they are a formidable energy sapping device.

Here are some examples of practical blocks:

- Household "do it yourself" jobs left undone

- Little or no help with difficult household chores

- Promises that are never kept with regard to jobs that you can't do yourself

Here are some examples of emotional blocks:

- Making small talk

- Listening to your partner talking rubbish

- Having to repeat yourself and having the same conversation over again because your partner does not listen to you when you are talking

- Trapped by friends who are needy all the time

- Suffering fools you don't know very well

- Agreeing with your partner when you really want to scream

- Trapped in your role as a major provider in the relationship

- Being aware of your negative repeating patterns and continuing to do them anyway

Practical blocks can be anything from a door that doesn't shut properly to a job you hate. The more blocks you suffer from, the more tired and sapped of energy you will become.

However, when you recognize and list your blocks and decide to do something about them, you will become totally aware of your current situation. You will regain your energy and become empowered. These acknowledgements will raise the quality of your life and you will become more confident. You are now starting your journey of self development.

The third key is to ask yourself, "What is my vision for my future?" First of all, what is a vision? A vision is what you want and where you want to be. The gap is the difference between where you are now and where you want to be. In order to fulfill your vision, you have to take responsibility for yourself and your life. Plodding along the same path isn't going to get you there. Instead, you have to change course and build your dream.

As outlined in the first key, you must take responsibility for yourself and your actions. To turn the vision into reality requires patience, endurance, strength, and a willingness to follow through despite possible and probable setbacks. Someone who takes responsibility is someone you can look up to and admire, not just for their achievements but for their attitude and the way they handle situations and people.

Problems will face you when you design your long-term strategy. To be able to move forward, it's necessary first to find out how to solve problems.

Ten Rules for good problem solving:

Rule #1: Good communication is essential in problem solving. Discuss issues in a positive way. Give each other the opportunity of talking without interruption. Do not point a finger at your partner. Instead, ask questions and invite cooperation in order to solve the problem being discussed. Be aware what words mean and how they can imply different things to different people.

Rule #2: Listen to what your partner is saying. Don't put your own interpretation on what you hear. If you don't understand it, restate it back as a question. Don't rush to solve the problem. Allow plenty of time to really look at the problem.

Rule #3: If either of you feel under pressure, take "time out" to release tension and stress during discussions. Agree on a suitable time to resume the discussion.

Rule #4: Be respectful and kind to each other. Learn to be objective rather than subjective. In other words, try to stay outside the problem to avoid your personal emotions getting in the way.

Rule #5: Work as a team. Don't fight each other, since you are both on the same side. Don't try to control the discussion.

Rule #6: Be creative in solving your problem. Ask yourselves, "How can we change the outcome of this problem so that it satisfies both of us?" Search for alternatives.

Rule #7: Work on one problem at a time. Don't confuse each other by dragging other problems into the discussion.

Rule #8: Brainstorm for possible solutions. Resist being judgmental of each other's suggestions. Fight fair and focus on the outcome.

Rule #9: Evaluate suggestions you have both made by writing down the disadvantages and advantages of each suggestion.

Rule #10: Don't let your problems rule your life. Remember, there is a solution for every problem, so find it.

These are the simple rules to stick to in order to undo a problem together.

Essential Needs for Productive Problem Solving

- A clear head
- An unbiased attitude
- Being non-judgmental
- Allow everyone to express their feelings
- Patience, tolerance and understanding
- Develop a clear description of the problem
- Take ownership of the problem
- Understand what will be the outcome if the problem is not solved
- Understand how the problem impacts on both partners and others
- Identify whether you or your partner, or both of you have the problem
- Identify the negative aspects of the problem
- Identify the positive aspects of the problem
- Identify how important the problem is and be able to prioritize the task of dealing with it

- Both must get involved and find different ways of handling the problem (brainstorming)

- Identify alternative approaches to the problem and follow through each alternative approach to is conclusion in order to see the consequences of each alternative

- Each of you must deal with the problem alone, finding ways to handle the issue. Then, share your answers with your partner. By doing this, each partner will feel valued and will gain self-respect in attempting to solve the problem alone. When you come together, both answers should be discussed to their ultimate conclusion and maybe a compromise of both answers is appropriate

- For good problem solving, it is important for each of you to face your part of the problem

- You should both be determined to follow through the problem to a mutually satisfactory conclusion.

"The essence of strategy is choosing what not to do. "

Michael Porter

8	**Devise a Short-Term Strategy**

What is a short-term strategy? It is a short-term plan of achievable goals. In order to be effective, your goals need to be:

- Realistic
- Attainable
- Measurable
- Prioritized
  - o What must be done;
  - o What may be done,
  - o What must not be done

Realistic

By realistic, I mean achievable and attainable. Setting unrealistic goals is both pointless and demoralizing. Set believable goals and save yourself a hard time. Break down your goals into smaller achievable targets. You will be able to achieve your bigger goals if you work on achieving smaller targets. It is very important to make your goals as realistic and achievable as you can.

Attainable

In order to proceed with this strategy, you have to take responsibility for yourself and your life. Your success in achieving your goals depends entirely on you. You wouldn't be reading this book if you already had what you wanted in life, were confident within yourself, happy, fulfilled and contented. So, do you believe enough in yourself and in what you can do to achieve your goals? Self-doubt and fear are huge obstacles you will come across on your way to a successful outcome.

Self-doubt may creep up on you without warning. One day you might be confident, assertive and capable—and almost overnight it would appear you have become less so. What happened?

You lurch from being an independent person to being unable to survive outside of a relationship. It doesn't even have to be a good relationship. Any relationship will do to validate you. You become dependent on your partner to make you feel OK. You feel worthless without having a lover/partner/ husband. This situation occurs when you lose focus on yourself.

The Romantic Myth

The "in love syndrome" fools you into believing you have everything that your heart desires. Being in love is an excuse to divert your attention from what you really want from life by believing that you have already got it. You become temporarily insane. It is wonderful to be in a loving relationship, but it needn't rob you of your individuality. Remember that your mate fell in love with the person you once were, not the robotic, emotional, dependent neurotic you have become.

Your conscious mind becomes totally absorbed by the new "love in your life," and you lose sight of everything else. Your conscious mind is filled with thoughts that occupy you and can control. On a subconscious level, everyone has things they want to achieve. But when your conscious mind believes you are happy, it blocks out all other thoughts. Your subconscious mind is filled with knowledge, information, experiences, observations, memories. Your unconscious mind holds deep-rooted beliefs, memories, instincts and well-established patterns of thought and behavior. Your unconscious mind also encompasses intuition.

Take time for yourself, sit down and make two columns.

1st column heading: The Problem
2nd column heading: The Outcome

You must now identify the problem and also the outcome you most want to achieve.

Next break down the problem by identifying small changes you can make to resolve issues you are facing. i.e.:

Practical Issue

Problem: I need a job. **Outcome:** Becoming employed

Targets

- Identify existing skills
- Research avenues of acquiring new skills, if necessary
- Register at Job Centre
- Look at daily newspaper for job opportunities
- Register at a Recruitment Centre
- Enquire at evening classes for appropriate learning opportunities

By doing these few tasks, you will feel empowered and reenergized. You are taking control and getting your life back.

Emotional Issue

Problem: Loss of power in a relationship. **Outcome:** Regaining power

Targets

- Be honest with yourself and identify where you are losing your power
- In your mind, take yourself through the pattern of your behavior that allows loss of your personal power

- Ask yourself what small thing you can change in order to retain some power. Take yourself back to the first step. Don't React—this step will help to change the behavior patterns in other people around you. Try it.

Remember to take one small step at a time. Don't react. Stay focused on the outcome you want to achieve. Don't spread yourself too thinly. Taking small steps allows you time to focus and gives you time for yourself, to learn and understand the process, and also to re-energize. You will be able to focus your energy on one target. The process will be slow, but stay in the moment and become dedicated to learning this new behavior. It will give you rewards. Persistence and patience are the keys to achieving your short-term goals, targets and eventual success. Remember, rarely will you achieve total success at your first attempt. If you did, there would be no need to build self-confidence and self belief.

Measurable

Learn to measure the small changes you make to your lifestyle and behavior. You can easily do this by taking stock of the circumstances, reviewing the situation and identifying how things have changed. By definition, something is measurable if it exists in distance, time, and form.

- What did you do to change the particular issue?
- What was the outcome of the change in pattern?
- Did it benefit you?
- Has it become calmer?
- Did the situation resolve itself more easily? etc.

These answers will clearly indicate the measure of your success so far.

Make One Small Change

When you embark on a journey of changing yourself, it is tempting to change everything about you all at once. In my experience, if you do this you will confuse yourself and all those people close to you. People will wonder what you are about. Why you have changed? What it is you want? More importantly, has the change got anything to do with them? They will become alert to the differences in you and this will lead them to becoming suspicious of your intentions.

In order for long-term change to be successful, you have to discipline yourself and not be tempted by the "too much too soon" scenario. Changes need to be subtle as they allow for a more positive and powerful view of your behavior.

There are different ways to change your ritual/routine, either by adding or removing steps that you always take. Another simple and effective method of changing patterns is based on the rule: "Never engage in any activity unless you would feel comfortable about telling at least two people of your intentions." If you are unable to do this, it is more likely that it is not a good thing for you to do. This rule is a kind of checklist that ensures your motives for the change are positive.

Negativity abounds when you are dealing with difficult situations,. It can permeate through nearly everything. It's important at this stage to examine your thoughts and to remember that it's the way you handle them that determines your mood and behavior. You might accept the thoughts in your mind as true and honest, but this is not always the case. A good way to change negative thoughts is to:

Challenge their accuracy by seeing the thought through someone else's eyes.

- Ask yourself how your parent would respond to the thought?

- Ask yourself how your best friend would respond to the thought?

- Ask yourself how would the person you most admire respond?

Thoughts that support your belief about your strengths, choices and optimism provide a basis for changes in attitudes, moods and behavior patterns. An essential part of creating a long-term strategy of change in your behavior patterns is by identifying and changing negative thought patterns. Thoughts can be changed by first of all identifying them, assessing their accuracy, dismissing them as of no real consequence, and turning the thought around. All these methods will assist you in changing your thought patterns and subsequent behavior.

It is important to identify, challenge and change your negative thought patterns. Changing your thought from negative to positive will help change your attitude, behavior and emotions. For example,

- **Negative thought**—I am useless, I can't do anything.

- **Positive thought**—I am useful, I can do many things.

But this is no use if it's just a mantra, said without belief. Better: 'I made a mistake here, but I have done many good things too. What can I learn from this mistake?'

Another simple change in behavior could be not responding to a question directly asked of you, but perhaps asking a question in return. In other words, throw the ball back into your partner's court. When quarrels occur, questions are asked, and the answers given are seen as important and vital to the outcome of the situation. So, if you give the wrong answer, the problem can get worse. However, if you answer the question, with a question, you not only remove yourself from the confrontation of the moment, and maybe defuse the situation slightly, but you are on a mission to learn exactly what it is the other person is getting at.

Small but significant changes can alter and lighten problems. i.e.,

Quarrel:

- He says: "How do you see this relationship going?"

- She says: "I think it's all downhill—you don't listen to me or do anything I ask of you."(A typical response and one uttered by many).

By answering the question in this way you are adding fuel to the fire by challenging and criticizing your partner.

Quarrel:

- He says: "How do you see this relationship going?"

- She says: "I haven't really thought about it—how do you see the relationship progressing?"

By using this approach and putting the ball firmly back in your partner's court, you are fact-finding to identify what your partner sees wrong in the relationship. By doing this, you will know more of how your partner feels and, therefore, not only give a more satisfactory response, but you will have more time to think out a constructive answer.

Your partner might respond by totally destroying the structure of your relationship. It is then up to you to decide if you want to go down that road or deflect your partner's intention and mood by adopting a different stance. If, for instance your partner starts pulling your relationship apart, you could answer that you need time to think things through as it's too important an issue to discuss from the top of your head. Again, what you are doing is giving yourself and the other person more time.

Moods change quite swiftly, and you could find that you will never need to answer the question because the mood has changed. The time you have allowed to pass has diluted the problem. I have counseled many people who experience problems after their partner has been drinking or taken drugs. You will never resolve an issue when in this situation, so what's the point in having the discussion at this time? Far better to diffuse the situation, by changing the subject, giving stock banal answers, until a more appropriate time when both of you are clear headed.

I must state that, in my experience, spontaneous reactions can only lead on to more problems. So think carefully and clearly before you make rash statements. This is one small way you can change the outcome and empower yourself at the same time. What you are actually doing is taking control of the situation.

> "The key to success is not through achievement but through enthusiasm."
>
> —Malcolm Forbes

9 | Observe, Consolidate, & Review

Observe

The next step in this system is to observe yourself and others around you. The act of making one small change in your behavior has an effect on those close to you. They can't pinpoint the change—it's too subtle. At first they might think they are imagining the change in you. They begin to see you differently. They might not like the change. In fact it's highly likely that they won't, particularly if that one small change has a consequence for them.

The one small change you make in your reactions to situations has a catapult effect on the other person, who then has to change the way to respond to you. Generally, people find any change in situations unsettling and confusing. Once you've made that one small change, continually practice it in appropriate situations. Do no more—just watch yourself and observe the responses of others.

- Did the situation turn around when you made that one small change?
- Did the situation stop when you made that one small change?
- Did it provoke an aggressive response?
- Did it provoke a more reasonable response?
- Did you feel in control of the situation?
- Did you feel out of control of the situation?
- Did you feel more able to continue the discussion after making the change?

These are some of the questions to ask yourself after making one small change in your behavior. Answer them honestly and adapt your behavior according to the outcomes you experienced. You could consider other responses. Sit down, think, and write a few responses you could use in your notebook for future reference. If you get stuck, go back and ask yourself how someone else would respond and use their ideas. Alternatively you could seek help from a friend or relative you know you can trust.

Changing behavior patterns for a more positive outcome in problematic situations is difficult to achieve at first. But with practice, it gets easier and your responses will become fluid and firmly established as a good habit. You must, however, take stock of your changing patterns from time to time.

If you are happy that you have achieved a result with the one small change you have made, don't be tempted to make another yet. This is very important. We all want to change too quickly and too soon. If you do this, you will falter on your path of change and eventually give up trying. This time of observation is important to firmly establish your responses in difficult situations.

Consolidate

In my own personal experience, I believe that it is important to take time between making changes to consolidate your newly found position—even though you might feel that does not amount to much yet.

- You need "time out" to evaluate our position within relationships

- You need time to judge accurately if you are on the right road to changing

- You will need to identify that the responses you have made suits you and fits nicely within you.

This period of consolidation help you to become more self-aware and gives you time to consolidate your new habit structures. You constantly need to reassess where you are and remember where you want to go. Don't forget that these steps lead you to your desired goal.

During this time, reflect on difficult situations you have experienced since starting these steps of change. If you have used your notebook (see p. 67) correctly, you will have all the information in it that you will need to accomplish this task. Go through your notebook and remember the situations and difficulties you have gone through. Are you satisfied with your reactions at that time? Is there room for improvement?

In your mind, see yourself in the situation again and change your response—trying something new and different—and imagine the outcome. I remind patients during counseling sessions that no one knows their partner or family member better than they do. Open your mind to how you think they would react to the different changes you are contemplating before putting them into practice. If you think hard enough, you will know instinctively how they would respond to the changes you are experimenting with.

All changes are difficult to make. To learn to change is a skill, and a skill is the ability to initiate, perform and complete difficult tasks. Make a habit of recording your achievements in your notebook. This simple but disciplined task will help you during the negative periods you will experience. Having time to consolidate your new habit gives you a break from becoming totally absorbed in the change process.

Changing life-long patterns is extremely tiring because you have to remain alert and focused at all times. You need this time of consolidation to give you time to "just be." Enjoy this time. You have adopted one small change in your pattern of behavior and now you need to reenergize your mind and body, and also relax. Learn to have quiet times. Easier said than done—I know—it took me years to learn this seemingly small quest. Read a novel, join an evening class, go for a drive in the car, go on a long walk, have a night out with friends or just take yourself off to your bedroom, lie down on the bed, close your eyes and think of something that makes you happy. Do something for yourself. Just relax into the moment.

> "This is the secret—the repertoire. You have to try to consolidate your repertoire. It is a big step if you know how to do that."
> —Cecilia Bartoli

Review

By now you have made one small change only. This might not seem a lot to you yet. Essentially you have learned how to:

- Discipline your thoughts
- Control your thoughts, reactions and behavior
- Not react
- Stay focused
- Reassess your situation
- Eliminate negative repeating patterns
- Stopped wasting your time and energy repeating the same strategy
- Explore other responses you could make in situations
- Practice your responses to situations
- Record your emotions and behavior in your notebook
- Evaluate the outcome you have achieved
- Be still within yourself and just simply "be."

Positive outcomes after changing

I hope by now you have seen the benefit of this strategy to help you change from a victim into an independent, empowered individual. That one small change you made is now well and truly part of your good habit strategy.

You took stock of your life by:

- Identifying what you wanted to change
- Preparing yourself to break lifelong patterns of behavior
- Not reacting spontaneously to situations
- Staying focused
- Developing a long term strategy
- Developing a short term strategy (achievable targets)
- Thinking through old responses
- Exploring and developing new ones
- Recording your emotions, thoughts and behavior in your notebook
- Practicing new habits
- Resisting the temptation inside you to change too much too soon.
- Taking time out for yourself in order to reenergize
- Evaluating outcomes you achieved

When itemized in this way, you should clearly see how much you have achieved so far. Tick the items you feel you have achieved.

Having completed this strategy myself, I learned that one small change in your behavior is enough to cope with mentally and physically for a period of up to three months before deciding on the next small change to make. This might seem too long at first. However, when you begin the strategy, you will quickly see the reason for allowing yourself this time in order to fully embrace the concept. You will understand that you are teaching yourself new habits, and adjusting to them. This takes discipline, focus, effort, practice. You will also have learned to accept that you won't always have a victory. Along the road to achieving your goal you will have failed, experienced negative feelings and wanted to give up. This is all normal. The most important fact is that you didn't give up and have achieved some success.

10 | Continue the Strategy

This is the final step! Having worked through this process, you must now decide if you are ready to work through these steps again.

Are you ready to make another small change in your thoughts and behavior?

By now, you should have fully adopted your first small change in behavior and thought.

Now you can make the second small change. The second small change could simply be changing your responses during confrontations/discussions/arguments etc. in previous chapters, I have already encouraged you to think about alternative responses you could adopt. Perhaps this would be a relatively easy change for you to make. You may have already put this into practice. If you have done this, and have had a positive result, that's fine. If not, you could do this now. Or think of the next step of change you would like to attempt.

I have tried several types of responses during this period in developing this strategy, ranging from agreeing with someone even if I don't agree with them to pretending I don't know the answer or to deliberately giving someone the answer I know they want. When I have confided to friends that I have done this, they commented that this is a weak thing for me to do. On the surface of it they are right. However, the subject matter involved when this has arisen has usually been unimportant to my emotional and financial circumstances, so why not? Peace at a small cost to me! You have to weigh the situation and circumstances as they presents themselves to you and draw your own conclusions.

I have used these steps in dealing with my own issues and also with countless numbers of patients I have counseled over a ten-year period. These changes are small, subtle and unobtrusive within a relationship and, because of this, there are immeasurable successes.

Your life's journey is often hard to deal with and we ask ourselves these questions:

- "Why is this happening to me?"
- "What have I done to deserve this?"
- "Am I such a bad person?"
- "How can I change my life around?"

The answer to these questions is:

- "It's happening to you because you have learned not to expect better."
- "You have done nothing wrong and don't deserve what is happening to you."
- "You are not a bad person."
- "You can change your life by focusing on new thoughts and ways to turn your life around."

You learn, early on in life, how to respond to different circumstances and situations.

You are conditioned by your role models and the environment you are raised in.

From this conditioning you learn good and bad habits that take you through your life. This outcome cannot be avoided. You are not responsible for the beliefs and behavior of your role models or for the environment you were raised in. You are, however, responsible and accountable for your beliefs, behavior and the environment you create for yourself today.

Don't look back and condemn or try to justify your past. Move on and create the life you deserve.

Personal Power

To have personal power is to have the ability to control your life and your future. You can only get personal power by being responsible and accountable for yourself. Personal power will only come to you when you have "let go" of old negative issues and repeating patterns. If you are unable to let go your pain of the past, you will forever be a prisoner of your own making. Being able to let go is a sign of power within.

Here are some examples of other ways to get personal power:

- By having a positive mental attitude

- From the love you get from your partner/parents

- By living a healthy life with a good diet and exercise regime.

Your power will increase when you feel good about yourself. Your self-belief, self-worth and self-respect are the foundation stones of personal power. Personal power is an outward sign that you are happy with yourself. When you have gained or regained your personal power, you will be able to organize/control/lead yourself and your partner/family/friends. Personal power will enable you to stand up for yourself and not accept being put down by others. You will learn that if something isn't appropriate, it is inappropriate, and your interaction to others will be guided by this type of basic, fundamental knowledge. To have gained personal power is an indication of your strength of character that has enabled you to survive difficult situations.

Power should not be taken from your partner or anyone else. To steal power from another person is to rob them of their energy. Healthy power is power from within and not power that you have acquired by negative means. In any form of communication between a couple, both should give an equal amount of energy/power into the discussion. If only one person uses their energy and power, this is an unequal interaction and the discussion should be discontinued.

The strategy outlined in this book is constructed for you to become powerful. Learning the skills required in my strategy will enable you to create a better life and will be significant in changing your role from victim to survivor. Learning to have a greater understanding of your partner's point of view will increase your awareness and stand you in good stead when dealing with family and friends and other people. Learning not to jump in "where angels fear to tread" is to learn diplomacy and patience, which are two of the essential tools of power.

Practicing the strategy will further develop your personality and character and will address "ego led" arguments. Ego-led arguments are unimportant, but you are unable to move on from them because you don't want to lose the argument at any cost. Try and remember old sayings, such as, "a still tongue keeps a wise head," "empty vessels make the most noise," '"fools rush in where angels fear to tread." These are all examples of speaking too much without thinking through things first.

Powerful people retain their power by listening without spontaneous reaction; by thinking through issues rather than saying the first thing that comes into your head. Powerful people are non-judgmental and flexible in their approach to others. Being able to take all this on board and acting on it will change the way you see yourself and will change the way others perceive you.

Personal Power from What You Have Learned...

- to let go of past hurt
- not to be judgmental
- to be understanding
- to be flexible
- to listen

- to think before you speak
- to be assertive rather than being weak, arrogant, or aggressive
- to be able to move on from the past
- to be realistic
- to have self-control
- that you have unlimited inner resources and potential

If you are able to tick most of the above, you have worked successfully through your emotions and released your old belief system and negative repeating patterns. You have learned to undo your negative conditioning and this has set you free from bad ideas and self perceptions that you had automatically adopted from your role models.

> "I am not interested in power for power's sake, but I'm interested in power that is moral, that is right and that is good."
>
> Martin Luther King, Jr.

"Victim" – A Poem

I am a victim
When did it start?
I cannot remember
The change in my heart

I know I am difficult
I know I am sad
The black shroud of fear
Is driving me mad

I want to trust you
I want to let go
I want to be able
To love myself more

I long to be free
Of emotional pain
To live life with abandon—
Once again

To be able to live
I can't wait for the time
I am able to forgive
Myself for my crimes

Forgive myself for all that I am
And surrender to life as best as I can

Appendix A: Bullying in the workplace

Bullying is perceived as acts or spoken comments that are meant to hurt and/or isolate you at work. It is when someone's behavior is offensive, for example: making sexual comments, abusing someone on the basis of race, religion, sexual orientation, disability, or age.

Here are some examples of what you will feel if you are being bullied:

- humiliated
- embarrassed
- offended
- intimidated
- belittled
- frightened

What Workplace Bullies Do

- exclude or isolate you
- deliberately undermines you
- physical abuse
- spread gossip about you
- set objectives that are impossible to reach
- make fun of you
- deliberately give you wrong information, thereby ensuring that you will make a fool of yourself
- use bad language against you
- block all promotion possibilities
- treat you unfairly more often than not
- blame you if things go wrong

I am sure you can add to this list.

What Impact Does Bullying Have On You?

Here are some examples:
- feelings of frustration
- make you angry
- make you vulnerable
- loss of confidence
- insomnia
- panic attacks
- depressed and/or anxious
- psychosomatic illnesses (headaches, etc.)
- tension at home
- demotivating
- unplanned time off work (phoning in sick)

Make your own list. I am sure you can add to mine. Bullies are most likely to pick on people who are non-confrontational, sensitive and dedicated to their work.

How Do You Spot a Bully?

Here are some examples:
- Bullies are critics; they find fault with everything
- Bullies set unrealistic goals
- Bullies want to control you
- Bullies humiliate and embarrass you
- Bullies are attention seekers
- Bullies are usually liars. They excel at deception
- Bullies sometimes use charm to catch their prey
- Bullies are emotionally immature
- Bullies are opinionated
- Bullies rarely give a straight answer
- Bullies feel superior

Workplace bullying is the torment of one adult by another. Bullies prey on sensitive, inadequate people and exercise power over them. Bullies usually start bullying in the schoolyard and will continue this practice in the workforce.

What Can You Do If You Are a Victim?

- Confront the bully and tell this person that the behavior is unacceptable and ask them to stop. It is preferable to do this with a witness present (even better if the witness is a union representative)

- Start keeping a daily diary of when, how and where the bullying takes place. This exercise will help you see if there is a particular pattern to the bullying. This diary is the evidence that may be required at a later date should the bullying not stop and you have to take it further

- Workplaces should have a bullying policy and should have a named person to report the bullying to. Make a formal complaint about the bully

- Should you have no positive result from reporting the bullying to the identified person on the policy, do not hesitate to go the next level of superiority

- Keep any memos and letters that can substantiate your complaint

Jack was a Store Manager and a first class serial bully. He regularly picked on his staff, particularly those people he found to be easily intimidated. Jack would keep up his bullying tactics until his victim resigned their employment with the Store.

Jack's persona was that of a charmer and using his charm techniques he would lure his victim into his web before employing his bullying ways. He thought nothing of marginalizing his victims to stop them challenging his authority and his decisions. Jack was cunning in that he would ask his staff for their observations and suggestions, but would then dismiss anything that did not fit into his criteria of managing. He was a poor communicator and therefore a bad manager. He was not a team player and could not motivate people in order to get the best out of them.

Inevitably, the stores he managed were unsuccessful, and because of this he was moved from store to store without higher management looking at why the stores he managed deteriorated. This pattern repeated itself many times before higher management recognized that the fault was with Jack and not the other employees. He was eventually demoted to managing smaller stores. His final move was to manage a toy store.

When Jack arrived at the toy store, everyone accepted him and believed that he was a really nice guy. However, the honeymoon period didn't last long and Jack was back to his old tricks ignoring some staff, aggressive with others and intimidating the weakest employees into submission. Diane had worked in the toy store for five years prior to Jack taking over as manager. Her work record was excellent and she was promoted to Assistant Manager just before Jack joined the store.

Jack soon learned Diane's weaknesses by discovering that behind her confident exterior lay a vulnerable, sensitive individual. Jack capitalized on these characteristics and hounded her by shouting at her and watching her every move. If she made a suggestion he would immediately dismiss it as rubbish. Needless to say, before very long Diane was taking time off work complaining that she was sick.

The Shop Steward called at Diane's home during one of her sick leaves from work and asked her what the problem was, and was there anything he could do to help her. He had known Diane for about two years and had been surprised that she was taking time off on sick leave and was curious to find out why this was happening. Diane confided in the Shop Steward and a complaint was made against Jack. When approached with this complaint, Jack immediately apologized to Diane and then backed off for a while to let the dust settle. This didn't last very long, however, and soon he was back to his old tactics. This resulted in Diane becoming stressed out and she started having panic attacks at work. Jack capitalized on her distress and suggested she resigned as the job was obviously too much for her. Diane lived with this tormenting behavior for over a year before she eventually caved in and left the Store. Jack is still employed by the toy store.

Appendix B: Emergency Contacts

International Contacts:

1-800-THERAPIST (1-800-843-7274)	1-800-843-7274
Find-a-Therapist.com	1.866.450.3463
POWA Helpline	(011)642-4345
The American Domestic Violence Crisis Line	866-USWOMEN

In Canada:

Assaulted Women's Helpline	416-863-0511
Domestic Violence Hotline	1-800-799-7233
National Domestic Violence Hotline	1-800-363-9010

In Australia:

Domestic Violence Crisis Hotline (NSW)	1800 656 463
Domestic Violence Crisis Hotline (Northern Territory)	1800 019 116
Domestic Violence Crisis Hotline (Queensland)	1800 811 811
Domestic Violence Crisis Hotline (South Australia)	1800 800 098
Domestic Violence Crisis Hotline (Tasmania)	1800 633 937
Domestic Violence Crisis Hotline (Victoria)	1800 007 339

In the United Kingdom:

Action on Elder Abuse Hotline	0808 808 8141
Muslim Women's Help Line	0181 904 8193
National Domestic Violence Hotline	0808 2000 247
Northern Ireland Women's Aid Federation	(028) 90 331818

In the United States:

Asian Task Force against Domestic Violence Hotline	617-338-2355
Crisis Support Network	1-800-435-7276
National Domestic Violence Hotline	1-800-799-7233
Safe Horizon's Domestic Violence Hotline	800-621-4673
The American Domestic Violence Crisis Line	1-866-USWOMEN
The National Coalition Against Domestic Violence	303-839-1852

Bibliography

Davies, Laura (1992) *Allies in healing: When the person you love was sexually abused as a child* – San Francisco: Harper Perennial

Gray, John (1998) *Men are from Mars, Women are from Venus.* Harper Collins

Jeffers, Susan (2005). *End the Struggle and Dance With Life.* Hodder & Stoughton.

Jeffers, Susan (1987) *Feel the Fear and Do It Anyway*, USA 1988 – First Ballantine Edition

Lew, Mike (1988) *Victims no longer: Men recovering from incest and other sexual abuse* – Nevraumont Publishing

McKenna, Paul and Willbourn, Hugh (2006) - *I can mend your broken heart* –Bantam Press, an imprint of Transworld, a division of Random House

Norwood, Robin (1985) *Women who love too much,* New York Jeremy Tarcher, Inc., of the Putney Berkley Group

Norwood, Robin (1994) *Why Me, Why This, Why Now,* Random House

Pease, Allan and Barbara (2001) *Why Men Don't Listen and Women Can't Read Maps* - Orion Publishing Company

Randall, Peter (2001) *Bullying in Adulthood.* Routledge

Volkman, Marian (2005) *Life Skills: Improve the Quality of Your Life with Metapsychology.* Loving Healing Press: Ann Arbor, MI.

Index

Life After Your Lover Walks Out
Book #1 in the 10-Step Empowerment Series

Life After Your Lover Walks Out

A Practical Guide

LYNDA BEVAN

Your long-time partner has just walked out on you forever:

- Do you feel paralyzed or afraid to move on?

- Does the thought or sight of your old partner with someone else fill you with rage?

- Are you worried or anxious about how to get by financially on your own?

- Are you afraid to start another relationship with a new partner?

- Do you lack energy and motivation to do anything at all since the break-up?

- Do you spend a lot of time thinking how it might have been different?

If you answered **yes** to any of these, this book is for you!

Praise *for Life After Your Lover Walks Out*

"This is a well thought out, useful little book that is an excellent guide for those recovering from a broken, long-term relationship."
—Robert Rich, PhD, M.A.P.S., author of *Cancer: A Personal Challenge*

"An excellent tool to help persons move on after the end of a relationship. *Life After Your Lover Walks Out* highlights the common cognitive distortions and exaggerated emotions and urges the reader to examine their actions and how they perpetuate their feeling of loss. Through the use of introspective questions the book invites the reader to take a journey of self examination in order to accept the loss and to reengage in life." —Ian Landry, MA, MSW, Case Manager

Loving Healing Press

Loving Healing Press
5145 Pontiac Trail
Ann Arbor, MI 48105

Tollfree (888)761-6268

info@LovingHealing.com

Distributed by Ingram

First Edition 2006
trade/paper — 6"x9"
ISBN-13 978-1-932690-26-2
$14.95 Retail
Includes bibliography, resources, and index.
For general libraries.

Life After Betrayal
Book #2 in the 10-Step Empowerment Series

LYNDA BEVAN

Your long-time partner has just betrayed your relationship and everything you hold dear:

- Are you stuck trying to decide whether to move forward in your relationship or give up?

- Do you find yourself repeating old ways of behavior?

- Do you frequently talk about whose fault the betrayal was?

- Are you continually dealing with jealousy and control issues?

- Are you tired of being a victim?

- Do you spend a lot of time thinking how it might have been different?

If you answered **yes** to any of these, this book is for you!

Praise *for Life After Betrayal*

"In reading *Life After Betrayal: A Practical Guide*, you will discover the difference between loving someone because you need them, and needing someone because you love them. This is a straightforward, easy-to-read and put-in-action book." —Catherine Phelps, Reader Views

"Nowadays there are too many books about adult loving relationships, but they usually are generic and abstract descriptions. This book is different because it moves to specificity and provides concrete steps to overcome a disrupting episode in our lives." —Carlos J. Sanchez, MA, Family Therapist

Loving Healing Press
Ann Arbor, MI 48105

Tollfree (888)761-6268

info@LovingHealing.com

Distributed by Ingram

First Edition 2007
trade/paper — 6"x9"
ISBN-13 978-1-932690-26-2
$14.95 Retail
Includes bibliography, resources, and index.
For general libraries.

Exclusive offer for readers of *Life Without Bullying!*

Share the power of Loving Healing Press books
Order direct from the publisher with this form and save!

Order Form – 25% Discount Off List Price!

Ship To:

_____

Name

_____   _____/_____

Address   Card #   Expires

_____

Address   _____

                                                    Signature

_____   _____   **Life Skills** _____ x $13 = _____

City   State   **Lover Walks Out** _____ x $11 = _____

_____   **Life After Betrayal** _____ x $11 = _____

District   Country   Zip/Post code

                                                    Subtotal = _____

_____

Daytime phone #   **Michigan Residents: 6% tax** = _____

_____   Shipping charge (see below) _____

email address   Your Total _$_____

Shipping price <u>per copy</u> via:

☐ Priority Mail (+ $3.50)   ☐ Int'l Airmail (+ $4)   ☐ USA MediaMail/4th Class (+ $2)

Fax Order Form back to (734)663-6861 or
Mail to LHP, 5145 Pontiac Trail, Ann Arbor, MI 48105

CPSIA information can be obtained at www.ICGtesting.com
Printed in the USA
LVOW041018170612

286481LV00006B/57/P